Disciple

Experience Drawing Closer to God and Fulfilling His Fruitful Plan for Your Life

Donald Mitchell

400 Year Project Press
Weston, Massachusetts
United States of America

400 Year Project Books by Donald Mitchell

Your Breakthroughs

2,000 Percent Living
Breakthrough Learning

The 2,000 Percent Nation

Help Wanted

Investigation Centers
Ways You Can Witness (with Cherie Hill, Roger de Brabant,
    Drew Dickens, Gael Torcise, Wendy Lobos, Herpha Jane
    Obod, and Gisele Umugiraneza)
Witnessing Made Easy (with Bishop Dale Combs, Lisa Combs,
    Jim Barbarossa, and Carla Barbarossa)

The 2,000 Percent Solution (with Carol Coles and Robert Metz)
The 2,000 Percent Solution Workbook (with Carol Coles)
The Portable 2,000 Percent Solution (with Carol Coles)
The 2,000 Percent Squared Solution (with Carol Coles)
Excellent Leadership
Excellent Solutions (For-Profit and Nonprofit Editions)

Business Basics

Advanced Business
Advanced Business for Innovation
Advanced Business for Social Benefits

The Irresistible Growth Enterprise (with Carol Coles)
The Ultimate Competitive Advantage (with Carol Coles)

Adventures of an Optimist

Disciple
Experience Drawing Closer to God and Fulfilling His Fruitful Plan for Your Life

ISBN: 978-0692903575
0692903577

For information, contact:

**Donald W. Mitchell
400 Year Project Press
P.O. Box 302
Weston, Massachusetts 02493
781-647-4211**

Published in the United States of America

This book is dedicated to:

Those who have accepted Jesus Christ
as their Lord and Savior,
want to experience God more fully,
desire to live the Gospel,
seek to draw closer to God, and
intend to help increase and improve God's Kingdom

May quickly and easily learning and applying
Godly lessons always be ahead of them!

And their spouses, their children and grandchildren,
and their descendants

May this book help them to always focus
on the Lord and doing His will!

Contents

Acknowledgments

Oh, give thanks to the LORD!
Call upon His name;
Make known His deeds among the peoples!

— 1 Chronicles 16:8 (NKJV)

I thank Almighty God, our Heavenly Father, for creating the universe and all the people on the Earth; our Lord and Savior, Jesus Christ, for providing the way for us to gain Salvation; and the Holy Spirit for guiding our daily paths towards repentance and righteousness. I also humbly acknowledge the perfect guidance I was sent from God through the Holy Spirit and His Word to write this book. I regret that as an imperfect being I undoubtedly misheard, misunderstood, and misapplied some of that perfect guidance.

I graciously acknowledge all those believers who have poured into me their love, knowledge, concern, and guidance. Those who have helped me are too numerous to mention here, but I am deeply grateful to each one.

I especially appreciate having learned much about becoming a disciple through studying with Pastor Doug Whallon of Grace Chapel in Lexington, Massachusetts. He has provided me with great Godly wisdom and described helpful examples of what and what *not* to do. I especially appreciate those at Grace Chapel who took my course based on this text while it was being finalized. I am also thankful for learning about his work with Pastor Muriithi Wanjau of Mavuno Church and Nairobi Chapel in Kenya, whose *Mizizi* workbook helped me learn a great deal about myself and boosted my faith.

I can never thank my family enough for allowing me the time and peace to work on such a huge and awe-inspiring project for God. They made many sacrifices without complaining and have been a continual source of inspiration.

I appreciate my many clients and students who held off on their demands for my help so that this project could receive the attention it required. Their financial support also made it possible for me to give this time to the Lord and to make this book available.

Finally, I am most appreciative of the many fine improvements that my editor, Bernice Pettinato, made in the text. This is the twenty-second book where she has helped me to make the messages clearer and more pleasant to read. As always, she was a delight to work with. Her kindness made the writing much easier. I value all she has taught me about writing. I look forward to learning new lessons from her during any future books.

I accept sole responsibility for any remaining errors and apologize to God and my readers for any difficulties and inconveniences that they encounter as a consequence.

Introduction

Experience God More Fully,
Live the Gospel,
Draw Closer to God, and
Help Expand and Improve God's Kingdom

Then He taught them many things by parables,
and said to them in His teaching:

"Listen! Behold, a sower went out to sow.

"And it happened, as he sowed,
that some seed fell by the wayside; and
the birds of the air came and devoured it.

"Some fell on stony ground, where it did not have much earth,
and immediately it sprang up because it had no depth of earth.
But when the sun was up it was scorched,
and because it had no root it withered away.

"And some seed fell among thorns;
and the thorns grew up and choked it, and it yielded no crop.

"But other seed fell on good ground and
yielded a crop that sprang up, increased and produced:
some thirtyfold, some sixty, and some a hundred."

And He said to them, "He who has ears to hear, let him hear!"

— Mark 4:2-9 (NKJV)

In this often-cited parable, Jesus taught how the fruitfulness (spiritual benefits) of someone sharing parts of God's Word (as are now found in the Bible) depends on those who hear the Word accepting and doing what It says (for more on this point, Jesus' explanation of the parable's meaning can be found in Mark 4:13-20, NKJV). When those who hear the Word obey, their lives become exponentially more fruitful, both through the sharers more often taking fruitful actions, as well as from a greater number of fruitful actions being taken by believers who have been influenced by the sharers' faithful words and deeds.

While teaching believers about what the Bible calls for us to do, I have always been struck by how frequently at least some parts the Word haven't been fully accepted and followed. Such lacks of acceptance and related disobedience have usually appeared to be connected, at least in part, to the believers then having had a too limited relationship with Jesus. I derive that observation from having heard such people talk about their relationships with Him.

While I am delighted to note that many wonderful books and resources can help acquaint someone with and deepen understanding of God's Word, I am dismayed to see that most of such sources provide relatively little assistance with directly building a believer's relationship with our Heavenly Father, the Lord Jesus Christ, and the Holy Spirit. By primarily acquiring such "head" knowledge, "heart"-based beliefs and actions based on a spiritually healthy relationship might not increase as much as God intends.

I feel called by God to write this book so that believers will better know and spend more fruitful time with our Heavenly Father, His Son Jesus, and the Holy Spirit through experiencing and interacting with each One more intimately, more often, and in more ways. As a result of reading and applying *Disciple*, believers will gain opportunities to greatly increase how often and deeply they notice and are affected by God's communications, touches on their lives, and handiwork around them. Hopefully, such new and increased experiences will then lead to a lifetime of drawing closer to God and growing spiritually in ways that lead to taking ever more fruitful actions.

In following this calling for preparing *Disciple*, I feel especially informed by a newly increased appreciation for the significance of the following words of Jesus that I have italicized from the Great Commission: "*teaching them to observe all things that I have commanded you.*" The entire Great Commission is quoted here:

> And Jesus came and spoke to them, saying, "All authority has been given to Me in heaven and on earth. Go therefore and make disciples of all the nations, baptizing them in the name of the Father and of the Son and of the Holy Spirit, teaching them to observe all things that I have commanded you; and lo, I am with you always, *even* to the end of the age." (Matthew 28:18-20, NKJV)

As you can see from these verses, helping people to accept Jesus as Lord and Savior isn't the only goal of the Great Commission. Such acceptance should also be seen as an essential first step towards creating a fruitful life with Jesus as a result of understanding and following His commands, another primary aspect of the Great Commission's direction. Note especially that these verses indicate that Jesus is present with us as we think and perform ("observe" in this translation) all that He has commanded us to do, an important fruit of the relationship that Jesus wants to have with each believer.

As we build our relationship with Jesus, we will want to, and actually will, do more of what He has already commanded *and* will command us to do. By more often acting in obedience to such commands, we will further build our relationships with Him and other believers. In addition, we will enjoy life more as we experience, observe, and reflect on the good that He has enabled us to help accomplish. What could be a more wonderful result?

As another part of our relationship with Jesus, believers are also commanded to serve those who need help in ways that are not necessarily aimed at the beneficiaries either gaining Salvation or developing a relationship with God. We see this direction in terms of serving other believers in Matthew 25:31-40 (NKJV), loving and serving nonbelievers (including those who are in rebellion against God) in Matthew 5:44-45 (NKJV), and being of assistance to anyone we come into contact with as demonstrated by the Parable of the Good Samaritan (Luke 10:25-37, NKJV, which is quoted in days three and four of week four of Part Two):

> "When the Son of Man comes in His glory, and all the holy angels with Him, then He will sit on the throne of His glory. All the nations will be gathered before Him, and He will separate them one from another, as a shepherd divides *his* sheep from the goats. And He will set the sheep on His right hand, but the goats on the left. Then the King will say to those on His right hand, 'Come, you blessed of My

Father, inherit the kingdom prepared for you from the foundation of the world: for I was hungry and you gave Me food; I was thirsty and you gave Me drink; I was a stranger and you took Me in; I *was* naked and you clothed Me; I was sick and you visited Me; I was in prison and you came to Me.'

"Then the righteous will answer Him, saying, 'Lord, when did we see You hungry and feed *You,* or thirsty and give *You* drink? When did we see You a stranger and take *You* in, or naked and clothe *You?* Or when did we see You sick, or in prison, and come to You?' And the King will answer and say to them, 'Assuredly, I say to you, inasmuch as you did *it* to one of the least of these My brethren, you did *it* to Me.'" (Matthew 25:31-40, NKJV)

" … [L]ove your enemies, bless those who curse you, do good to those who hate you, and pray for those who spitefully use you and persecute you, that you may be sons of your Father in heaven …." (Matthew 5:44-45, NKJV)

Thus, a believer's faithfulness in being a disciple can be discerned by the combination of his or her relationship with Jesus, obedience to Jesus' commands, and how she or he treats the most vulnerable. Some believers may be upset by considering this perspective, especially those who are currently doing little for the most vulnerable. For such individuals, however, this same information can be a bountiful source of joy after their relationships with Jesus more fully develop and their ability to care, sense of compassion, and desire to serve blossom by assisting those who greatly need help.

Let me explain how these observations about believers have helped to shape *Disciple.* The book's content is solely aimed at serving believers in Jesus. As a result, these teachings are not appropriate for either seekers or doubters.

If you aren't sure what it means to be a believer in Him, the first step is to repent (reject and turn away from) your sins (disobedience to and rebellion against God and His commandments, Mark 1:15, NKJV). After that, you must believe in Jesus being God's Son, who died for our sins and rose again on the third day, and accept Him as your Lord and Savior (Matthew 4:17 and John 3:7, NKJV). As a result, you will be born again (John 15:4, NKJV). Jesus directed you to be baptized as a way to witness to others your commitment to Him (Matthew 28:19-20, NKJV).

In serving believers, I have sought to provide sufficient head knowledge so that someone can better participate in the kind of relationship that our Heavenly Father, the Lord Jesus, and the Holy Spirit want to have with her or him, while also encouraging experiences that will greatly increase awareness of Them, desires to draw closer to Them, and yearnings to serve others in the name of Them. After these relationships are firmly established, believers can add other head knowledge beyond what is contained in *Disciple* through daily time spent in Bible study and contemplation, attending church services and activities, and prayer (each of which is encouraged by *Disciple*), actions that will help relationships with our Heavenly Father, the Lord Jesus, and the Holy Spirit and assist a believer to become more fruitful.

To accomplish these results, *Disciple* contains four parts: Experience God More Fully; Live the Gospel; Draw Closer to Our Heavenly Father, the Lord Jesus Christ, and the Holy Spirit; and Help Expand and Improve God's Kingdom. Each part can be studied separately from the others. It's also perfectly okay to take a break before starting another part, especially if you use the intervening time to more fully absorb and appreciate what has just been learned and experienced. I recommend, however, that the sequence of the parts in *Disciple* be followed.

Each part is designed to be studied and experienced over five weeks. Those who use the book individually are welcome to lengthen that time to make engagement with the material more convenient and extensive … and are especially encouraged to do so for the purpose of gaining more experiences with our Heavenly Father, the Lord Jesus Christ, and the Holy Spirit. However, do not shorten the time. Growing spiritually and in relationships is often slow and should not be rushed.

In suggesting this length of time for the study and experience of each part, I must note that some lessons and experiences may continue for longer times. Keep going on the longer-term tasks. Many of them are the ones that will help you the most.

The book can also be used by those teaching discipleship courses. In such an application, a weekly session of 60 to 90 minutes can be used by readers to share and discuss the contents of, their application experiences with, and their questions concerning *Disciple*. Some churches may wish to provide such a class for new believers and those who have not yet received much education about what it means to accept and follow Jesus as Lord and Savior. Such a course can either address the four parts at one time or be divided into four separate courses that occur over one to two years.

In addition, some more mature believers may want to help individual believers develop their knowledge of, faith in, and relationships with our Heavenly Father, the Lord Jesus Christ, and the Holy Spirit. *Disciple* can be used to serve this purpose, as well. Weekly one-on-one meetings to discuss the content, questions, and experiences will be useful supplements to studying and applying the book.

Each lesson within a part is intended to be covered over two or more days. I strongly recommend spending more than one day on a lesson due to my past discipleship students having told me that the study aspects of a discipleship course need to be as brief as possible each week. Consequently, I have reduced such weekly content by more than 60 percent from the amount contained in courses that I have taught and facilitated for such students. Having at least two days devoted to a topic also encourages engaging in more of the experiential dimensions of *Disciple*, potentially even allowing for repetition of experiences that a believer finds to be most enlightening and encouraging. If someone wanted to go slower and use a week or more on each lesson, such an approach could be even more beneficial.

For me, one of the most difficult, but most rewarding, parts of taking a discipleship class was memorizing Bible verses. After initial struggles, I finally gained the knack of doing so. Because of the benefits I gained as a result, I now occasionally add another verse to my repertoire.

I initially learned to do so by hand writing the verses on 3 x 5 cards, sticking the cards in my shirt pocket, and then reviewing the verses whenever I had a spare moment (such as while on hold waiting for a telephone conversation to begin). I memorized one word at a time, adding to my recollection and practice by just that one word a day. I later began to recite these verses during my prayers until they were even more deeply absorbed, and I have continued doing so. This learning process has continued to work best for me. Since then, my days have been enriched and better directed by the words from useful Bible verses popping into my head at appropriate times.

To encourage you to gain the same benefit, I have included one memory verse for each week. Knowing how hard it was for me to learn long verses, I have tried to find the shortest and easiest verses for you to memorize from among those that are most relevant to each week's lessons. I can also report having memorized all these verses, as well. If you need more than a week to memorize one of these verses, don't worry. Just keep repeating the verse until it is firmly in your mental grasp. You'll be glad that you did every time that a great verse comforts or directs you at a difficult or uncertain moment!

Disciple mostly quotes Matthew, Mark, Luke, and John. These selections are intentional. Jesus' words are concentrated in these four books of the Bible. I'm sure you want to know as much as you can about what He taught and commanded.

Having taken my own church's discipleship class nine times so far, I am mindful of how repetition has greatly increased my understanding of how to be in a relationship with our Heavenly Father, the Lord Jesus Christ, and the Holy Spirit and to be a disciple of Jesus, helped me draw closer to Them, and encouraged me to be active in more ways to expand (include more people) and improve (upgrade the fruitfulness of) God's Kingdom. I encourage all readers of *Disciple* to repeat their study and application of these materials on a regular basis, potentially as often as once a year. Doing so will make it easier for you to notice the new things that God wants to show and tell you!

I was encouraged to answer questions and make personal notes in a daily journal while taking my church's discipleship course. I am very glad that I did. I have kept that journal and frequently reread my comments. Doing so has helped me to mark the progress that I have made in becoming a better disciple of Christ. I particularly enjoy seeing the evolution in my responses to the questions encountered during the nine different occasions (so far) that I have taken the course.

Disciple encourages you to keep a daily journal to help you engage in more activities that will build your relationships with our Heavenly Father, the Lord Jesus Christ, and the Holy Spirit, such as noting the prayers you've made, how those prayers were answered, and what the results of any fulfilled prayers have been. As time passes and some longer-term impacts of those answers become more apparent, I'm sure you'll join me in being amazed by how much you didn't initially appreciate about how effectively your prayers have been addressed.

I have included simplified versions of Jesus' commands and statements that imply commands in Appendix A so that you can more easily become familiar with and follow them. To gain a deeper understanding, read the verses in several different translations. You will also find my personal testimony in Appendix B and a description of The 400 Year Project (research from 1995 through 2015 focused on increasing every aspect, from spiritual to tangible, of what each person on Earth accomplishes by at least 20 times, while using the same or less time, effort, and resources) in Appendix C. Through 2035, The 400 Year Project will be in the implementation phase of turning that research into day-to-day, effective practices that hopefully everyone uses.

Only our Heavenly Father, the Lord Jesus Christ, and the Holy Spirit know how *Disciple* will change your life. Since They have good plans for each of us (Jeremiah 29:11, NKJV), I'm sure that you will find being more closely aligned with Them to be an awesome and joyful experience … even should you encounter many difficulties while doing so. If you would like to share your experiences with applying the lessons in *Disciple*, I would be delighted to hear from you. Feel free to reach me by e-mail at donmitchell@fastforward400.com/.

Part One:

Experience God More Fully

"But he who received seed on the good ground is
he who hears the word and understands it,
who indeed bears fruit and produces:
some a hundredfold, some sixty, some thirty."

— Matthew 13:23 (NKJV)

In Part One, *Disciple* will draw your attention to aspects of God's influence that you either may not currently perceive or contemplate as often as you would benefit from so doing. Before you begin the first lesson, take a few moments to think about when, where, and how you have most intensely experienced being with God. I encourage you to note those experiences that come to mind in your journal or in the space below. Whenever you feel far from God, review these notes to remind you of His presence and His desire to be close to you. Repeat such experiences whenever you can!

Week One: Days One and Two

Contemplate Creation

Jesus said to him,

"'You shall love the LORD your God with
all your heart, with all your soul, and with all your mind.'
This is the first and great commandment."

— Matthew 22:37-38 (NKJV)

Matthew 22:37-38 (NKJV) describes what Jesus selected from among all the commandments in the Old Testament to highlight as the first and great commandment. I commend this commandment to you as your first memory verse: "You shall love the LORD your God with all your heart, with all your soul, and with all your mind" (Matthew 22:37, NKJV).

I have always been grateful, in part, to Jesus for His selection of this commandment because it is fairly easy to remember. However, whenever I sigh with relief over being able to recall it, I often then doubt that I can love God with all my heart, soul, and mind. Perhaps you have had a somewhat similar reaction on at least some occasions.

If so, relax. In this first part of *Disciple*, you will be directed to verses and experiences that will make you want to love God more, which can be repeated until you can do so with every aspect of your being. Here's the first of these helpful verses: "In the beginning God created the heavens and the earth" (Genesis 1:1, NKJV).

This verse tells us that everything tangible (such as a grain of sand, a beautiful flower, a tall tree, a mountain, the moon, or a distant star) and intangible (such as the laws of nature, a thought, or your spirit) was created by God. Clearly, contemplating the Creator of all such creations can leave us amazed, awe-struck, and inspired. Thinking about His creation is also very humbling in terms of considering the vast gap between His capacities and ours. I'm beyond being merely impressed, and I'm sure you are, as well.

The story gets even better. God didn't create the heavens and the Earth to amuse Himself. Instead, He created them for a purpose that included *you*, as we see in Genesis 1:28 (NKJV): "Then God blessed them, and God said to them, 'Be fruitful and multiply; fill the earth and subdue it; have dominion over the fish of the sea, over the birds of the air, and over every living thing that moves on the earth.'" In addition, other parts of Genesis indicate that the plants were provided by God to serve as our food.

So, everything you see is intended for your benefit! Isn't that amazing? Our natural response is to wholeheartedly praise and glorify God for His great creativity and generosity, as King David did in Psalm 8:1 (NKJV): "O Lord, our Lord, How excellent *is* Your name in all the earth, Who have set Your glory above the heavens!"

As scientists have learned and described more about how the physical world functions, believers' wonder at His creation has increased. For example, tiny subatomic particles provide universal building blocks to form the astonishing variety of every physical thing we see and experience. God can rearrange these particles to create whatever He wants, whenever He wants. As another cause for wonder, the conditions that allow life as we know it to flourish on the Earth are all but seemingly impossible to find anywhere else throughout the entire universe, beginning just a few miles above the Earth's surface. How blessed we are to have our world and the life-giving atmosphere that encompasses it! Further, the universe is not only so large that we cannot imagine its full extent, despite being able to attach immense numbers to describing these distances ... but the entire universe is also expanding at an astonishing rate, one that's even faster than what scientists believe occurred when the universe was first formed! Within the universe, the twinkling stars not only delight and guide us at night, but they continually turn gases into more complex elements that are ejected into space to help form new celestial bodies while also adding material to existing ones.

You undoubtedly have your own examples of how God's creation amazes and delights you. Write those examples in your journal whenever you think of one. As you do, leave some space so that you can easily add to the list.

As the second part of each lesson, you will answer questions designed to lead you through mental and physical experiences that will draw you closer to God. Feel free to engage in such experiences during both days of each lesson. You will gain even more benefits if you continue doing so after the two days. Below are some experiences for contemplating creation as a means of more accurately appreciating God.

Experience God More Fully by Contemplating Creation

Be sure to engage in at least one of these experiences before starting the next lesson. If you enjoy doing so, perform more of, vary, or repeat these experiences.

1. What can you observe when you look closer in studying a flower? Make notes about each aspect you notice. Try to find more than 50 different aspects. Then reflect on the intricacy, brilliance, and beauty of God's design. Jot down your reactions and thoughts. What do these observations tell you about God?

2. What do you notice when looking at the big picture by examining photographs of galaxies or clusters of stars, such as the Milky Way? Notice anything that strikes you as unusual about what you see. Then consider the grandeur and scope of God's creation. What do the objects in these images suggest to you about God?

3. What do you find when you simplify something into its bits and pieces, such as by opening a large seed, taking it apart, and examining its different parts? You may find it helpful to use a magnifying glass as you do. Then think about how God designed the seed to carry and nurture new life. How has God created you to do the same?

4. What do you see when you look beneath the surface? Go outdoors and pick up something that's been in place for some time, such as a large, flat rock. Notice what's beneath it. You'll probably find life that's been operating in the dark, contributing to God's plan of providing for all creation. If you don't find anything under the object, gently dig a hole there until something emerges. How does what you discovered affect your awareness of how extensive and complete God's influence is?

5. What can a new perspective reveal to you? Here's one example: Think about how the Earth appears as only a small dot when viewed through the camera of a satellite circling Saturn. Visit some familiar place or scene. However, this time find a new vantage point, such as a much higher or lower one ... and also look from a different angle that's to the right or left. How does the shift in perspective affect what you notice? What does the shift tell you about how you should perceive God?

6. What do the small forms of life tell us? Use a microscope to examine a drop of pond water. Consider how much life God has concentrated there. If you don't have access to a microscope, find a video of seeing the same on an Internet site or in a photograph in a book. What does God's work on a small scale tell you about His presence and attention?

7. What can carefully examining something you have never paid much attention to teach you? What do you notice for the first time? Why do you think God included those previously unnoticed aspects?

Week One Memory Verse

"You shall love the LORD your God with all your heart, with all your soul, and with all your mind." (Matthew 22:37, NKJV)

Week One: Days Three and Four

Be Thankful for God's Blessings

*"But seek first the kingdom of God and His righteousness,
and all these things shall be added to you."*

— Matthew 6:33 (NKJV)

In Matthew 6:33 (NKJV), Jesus pointed out that God provides the essentials that each person needs, such as food, liquids to drink, and clothing, much as He supplies whatever birds need to survive, for those who are focused on His Kingdom and righteousness. Rather than being concerned that our needs won't be met, our faith should grow to the point where we follow God's commands as our focus ... and trust Him to take care of providing our day-to-day needs.

If you find it hard to follow that direction, you aren't alone. Many believers spend much time worrying about, plotting, and adjusting how to produce some sought-for result that isn't connected to either expanding or improving God's Kingdom. Because of being so busy seeking the unconnected result, less time and effort are then applied to doing the work of the Kingdom.

Perhaps a different verse will increase your desire to follow God's priorities: "And God *is* able to make all grace abound toward you, that you, always having all sufficiency in all *things,* may have an abundance for every good work" (2 Corinthians 9:8, NKJV). Notice that this verse talks about being provided by God with *more than enough for our needs* **and** *to do every good work.* As a result, you could even receive more resources to do God's work by focusing first on performing His work and letting Him provide, than you would by spending time trying to generate more of such personal provision on your own before shifting your efforts to advancing His purposes.

Whether or not relying completely on God to meet your needs seems like something you are now able to do, your faith in Him as a provider will increase after considering what you have already received. Instead of doing so, most people mainly focus on what they don't have: something others have, a certain skill or talent, or some kind of status. Seen from the perspective of all the necessary and helpful people, wonderful things, superb abilities, and abundant resources that we have in our lives, such as life itself, the love that delights us, the beauty that abounds around us, the wonderful relationships we have developed, and how our needs have been faithfully met, many of such "missing" items seem trivial in comparison.

Experience God More Fully by Increasing Your Awareness of the Blessings He Has Provided

Some believers report astonishing shifts in their faith, happiness, satisfaction, love, and kindly feelings towards others from identifying as many as possible of the blessings that God has already provided to them and those they love. After considerable attention to the task, some people have reported finding more than a thousand of such blessings. Whether you find few or many, your perspective will never be the same after noticing and listing your God-given blessings. Some questions are provided below to help you start. Add other benefit dimensions that are important to you. Notice any future changes in the blessings you identified and add them to your journal ... and later list new blessings as you experience them. Note the little things, such as seeing the sun break through the clouds on a gloomy day, as well as the big ones, such as when God spared your life during an accident or healed you from an often-fatal disease. Here are questions to help you begin your list of God-given blessings:

1. What blessings has simply being alive brought you?

2. What blessings have caused you to smile?

3. What blessings have made you laugh?

4. What blessings have left you feeling peaceful?

5. What blessings have caused you to feel loving or loved?

6. What blessings have brought you satisfaction?

7. What blessings have made you feel more secure?

8. What blessings have surprised you in terms of God's great generosity?

9. What benefits will you gain if you continue listing new blessings every day?

Week One Memory Verse

"You shall love the LORD your God with all your heart, with all your soul, and with all your mind." (Matthew 22:37, NKJV)

Week One: Days Five and Six

List and Be in Awe of Your Fulfilled Prayers

So Jesus answered and said to them,
"Have faith in God. For assuredly, I say to you,
whoever says to this mountain,
'Be removed and be cast into the sea,' and
does not doubt in his heart, but believes
that those things he says will be done,
he will have whatever he says.
Therefore I say to you,
whatever things you ask when you pray,
believe that you receive them,
and you will have them."

— Mark 11:22-24 (NKJV)

God wants us to be aware that He is always seeking to draw closer to us by listening to and answering our prayers, as well as by fulfilling our prayer requests when they advance His Kingdom. Having such experiences should make us eager to draw closer to Him, to praise Him for His faithfulness, and to live in complete confidence that He is present and active on our behalf.

Yet sometimes our faith can be disturbed if we don't receive exactly what we ask for, just when we want it. Such a reaction is much like how some people respond when they don't like the service they receive at a once-favorite restaurant. In annoyance, such diners may not return, forgetting all the good service they had enjoyed on earlier occasions.

There are several reasons why our requests may not be fulfilled. Mark 11:22-24 (NKJV) tells us that we can undermine our prayers by not believing that the requests will be fulfilled. Other causes of God not honoring the request can relate to praying without having first repented of any sins and asked forgiveness, not first forgiving others, or even asking for something that's not good for us and others. Consider what the verses of Psalm 84:11-12 (NKJV) have to say on these points:

For the LORD God *is* a sun and shield;
The LORD will give grace and glory;
No good *thing* will He withhold
From those who walk uprightly.

O LORD of hosts,
Blessed *is* the man who trusts in You!

So, we should, instead, rejoice when God doesn't immediately fulfill our requests. He's simply providing a blessing by encouraging us to increase our faith and walk in righteousness (by repenting and asking forgiveness for sins), as well as by keeping us from receiving what is harmful to us and others.

In this lesson, however, our focus is on remembering God's faithfulness in having fulfilled our prayers.

Experience God More Fully by Appreciating His Faithfulness by Being in Awe of God's Provisions Resulting from Our Prayer Requests

Perhaps you already have a prayer journal in which you have written your past requests to God. If so, you can review those prayers now to consider how some of them have been fulfilled. While doing so, keep in mind that God may answer a prayer by providing exactly what is requested, delivering something better or different, replying "not now," or by simply saying "no." Where the initial answer was "not now," but the request was later fulfilled, note both answers.

If you do not have such a journal, I am sure this assignment will make you realize some good reasons for keeping one … especially for increasing your faith and drawing closer to God. If you would like to start one today, one approach is to first list what you pray for today. Then each day write down what answers you receive to these prayers and add any new prayers that you make to that day's entry. If God fulfills a request, note that, too, on the day that it occurs. You can also start by remembering any times when you seemed to have been in desperate circumstances and some version of "Help me, God!" was your prayer. In addition, you might look back on those occasions when you didn't think you could achieve some Godly result with either your own strength or skill and you asked God to help. How did He respond to help you in answer to such prayers? Of course, the most recent prayer requests that were fulfilled will be the easiest for you to recall. Your awareness of His presence and awe for His amazing character and faithfulness will probably increase as you consider the effects on your life. After doing so, make notes in your *Disciple* journal about what you learned from this review and what experiences led you to gain such understanding. Leave room to add new experiences and memories so that you can continue to build on your past experiences to better guide your future relationship with God. Here are specific questions to answer:

1. What prayer requests has God fulfilled?

2. How might your life have been different in the past and be changed now if God had not answered these prayers as He did?

3. What did you learn from these observations about what God has done?

If you found these activities to be helpful, start a prayer journal (if you don't already have one) so that you'll be more aware of your prayers and God's answers. Add to the journal daily your new prayers, God's answers, and the results of any fulfilled prayers. During week four of Part Three, we'll spend more time learning how to write and use such a journal. Feel free to read and apply that information now to make your initial efforts for a prayer journal more effective.

Week One Memory Verse

"You shall love the LORD your God with all your heart, with all your soul, and with all your mind." (Matthew 22:37, NKJV)

Week Two: Days One and Two

Identify Possible Benefits of Unfilled Prayer Requests

"Do not lay up for yourselves treasures on earth,
where moth and rust destroy and
where thieves break in and steal;
but lay up for yourselves treasures in heaven,
where neither moth nor rust destroys and
where thieves do not break in and steal.
For where your treasure is, there your heart will be also."

— Matthew 6:19-21 (NKJV)

God always sees the big picture. Because He does, you have probably noticed that He sometimes responds to your prayer requests by multiplying benefits beyond what you asked for to accomplish more for His Kingdom. For instance, you might have prayed to gain more knowledge of the Bible. One way He might have helped was by encouraging you to take some courses. As you did so, you may have met believers who showed you a great many new and more fruitful ways to act on your faith.

You may also have noticed that some believers who were undoubtedly praying for relief from suffering caused by the actions of others did not seem to receive any lasting benefits. Why might such a result occur? Let me introduce you to a pair of verses that may help your understanding:

"Blessed are you when they revile and persecute you, and say all kinds of evil against you falsely for My sake. Rejoice and be exceedingly glad, for great is your reward in heaven, for so they persecuted the prophets who were before you." (Matthew 5:11-12, NKJV)

While you might not initially be very happy to receive the treatment described in Matthew 5:11 (NKJV) if it happened to you, your reaction could change as you learned to set a good example for others. Because you stood up to the challenge, God will reward you in heaven, whether or not there is an Earthly reward. Consider, however, that experiencing such ill treatment can also help you to increase your faith, as you appreciate the strength that God gives you to bear the burden. As you undergo such experiences, you might better understand how Jesus may have felt while receiving the punishment that we deserve, punishment that included a humiliating and painful death for Him. As such understanding increases, undoubtedly you will draw closer to Jesus, a great blessing.

In this lesson, we are humbly reminded that we serve God and His purposes, not the reverse. To better appreciate our role in relation to God, we can consider what His intentions might have been in not answering our prayer requests in the ways that we had hoped. While doing so, it's important not to see such results as indicating that He doesn't love us, doesn't care, or is powerless to help. Instead, we need to identify and appreciate as many as possible of the effects on His Kingdom that His choices might have had with regard to our prayer requests. For these two days, we'll focus on doing so by considering what the previously unappreciated Kingdom and personal benefits of any delayed ("not now") or completely refused ("no") prayer requests might have been.

Experience God More Fully by Considering Possible Kingdom and Personal Benefits of Your Prayer Requests Not Being Fulfilled

At first, finding such possibilities might feel quite challenging. After all, only God knows why He did what He did. How can we possibly determine His reasons? Well, we can ask Him for guidance. While He may not choose to explain the reasons for what has not yet occurred, surely He will not withhold perspectives about His denials that can increase our faith and draw us closer to Him.

A little practice in shifting perspectives can also help. Think about some horrible event that could not possibly have created any benefits for anyone. For instance, the tragic deaths from the sinking of the ocean liner *Titanic* might come to mind. Surely some of the passengers prayed before leaving England that they would have a safe and pleasant voyage. Yet no one did. I often imagine passengers and crew drowning in the dark, icy waters of the North Atlantic. Many lives were lost that could have been saved if sufficient lifeboats had been present, boarded, and launched in a timely manner.

Let's look for some positive consequences of the sinking. As an example, this tragedy did a great deal to cause nations to require that ships carry sufficient lifeboats for all passengers and crew, and that the crews do more to keep passengers safe. As a result, how many lives have been extended since then for people who became born again after surviving a sinking? How many other believers have not perished in ship accidents and then used the rest of their lives to act more fruitfully to increase and improve God's Kingdom? Surely, these life extensions served God's purposes in at least such ways. While it can be harder to imagine any personal benefits, one possibility is that at least a few of those who died in the sinking had been harming others and wouldn't have stopped doing so. If that possibility is true, then some survivors (and those who had been affected by the wrong-doers, but who were not on board) could have gained some personal benefits.

One way to gather potential insights into God's purposes is to ask, "What's good about what happened?" While at first you may think of nothing, eventually the Holy Spirit may reveal something important to you. Listed below are some questions that may help you consider how your unfilled prayer requests could have actually brought Kingdom and personal benefits for some. Ask these questions about each of your unfilled prayer requests and note the answers in your *Disciple* journal:

1. What's good about the results of God not having provided what I prayed for that was intended to help others?

2. What's good about the results of God not having provided what I prayed for that was intended to help me?

3. What Kingdom benefits might have been created as a result?

4. What personal benefits for others might have been experienced?

5. What personal benefits for me might have been created?

6. What beneficial opportunities became available that someone else could have engaged in, but didn't?

Week Two Memory Verse

"… [L]ay up for yourselves treasures in heaven …." (Matthew 6:20, NKJV)

Week Two: Days Three and Four

Consider Why God Might Have
Created Your Characteristics

For You formed my inward parts;
You covered me in my mother's womb.
I will praise You, for I am fearfully and wonderfully made;
Marvelous are Your works,
And that my soul knows very well.
My frame was not hidden from You,
When I was made in secret,
And skillfully wrought in the lowest parts of the earth.
Your eyes saw my substance, being yet unformed.
And in Your book they all were written,
The days fashioned for me,
When as yet there were none of them.
How precious also are Your thoughts to me, O God!
How great is the sum of them!

— Psalm 139:13-17 (NKJV)

For those who are not familiar with these verses, it can be surprising to first realize that how we were uniquely formed, both mentally and physically, reflects some of God's purposes for our relationship with Him and for increasing and improving His Kingdom.

Regardless of your prior awareness of God's influence on your life in such ways, think about what can be deduced about God's good plan for you by considering your characteristics and how they have affected your life so far. For instance, what temptations are you easily able to resist because they have little or no appeal to you? Perhaps God intended you to serve His Kingdom in places where such temptations are overwhelming for most other believers.

Is your body quite different from many other people? How does such a difference enable you to come into friendly contacts with certain people more often than others? How have such contacts affected your spiritual development and your fruitfulness?

How have your physical characteristics enabled you to participate in some activities, but not in others? What have been some of the spiritual and fruitfulness consequences so far?

How are you similar to most other people? In what ways does being so increase your ability to understand and connect with others in ways that increase your and their connections to God?

As you can see from these questions, God's intentions for us are exhibited for all to see or experience through how we appear, what we can do well or poorly, and how our hearts, minds, and emotions operate. Because God has specific intentions in mind for each individual, appreciate that you have been created to be exactly the way that He wants. Keep hold of that thought the next time you are tempted to feel unhappy because you lack enough of some attribute to accomplish one of "your" intentions. When you have such a reaction, realize, instead, that God's intentions are probably different. Such a thought will help you to stay oriented towards what He wants you to do. For example, if you lack some skill, but feel called to apply it by Him, such a lack might be part of God's intention for helping you become and remain more humble and for giving you good reasons to rely more on Him. Or, perhaps God doesn't want you to be distracted, and lacking the skill helps you focus on doing what He wants in other ways.

Experience God More Fully by Examining How You Were Formed Demonstrates Part of God's Purposes for Your Life

If you aren't sure how to begin such an examination, you might ask those who know you best what they find to be most distinctive about you physically, emotionally, and mentally. You might also find it helpful to observe others as you go about your daily activities with an eye to noting how they differ from you in various ways. Doing so can help you notice more of your own distinctiveness. Here are questions designed to take you further in examining yourself to identify more of God's purposes for your life:

1. What temptations are you easily able to resist, and what have been the consequences for your spiritual development and service for expanding and improving God's Kingdom?

2. What temptations are you *not* easily able to resist, and what have been the consequences for your spiritual development and service to God's Kingdom?

3. How do your physical characteristics affect what activities you do and with whom you most frequently come into contact, and what have been the consequences for your spiritual development and service for expanding and improving God's Kingdom?

4. How does the way your mind works affect what activities you do and with whom you most frequently come into contact, and what have been the consequences for your spiritual development and for enhancing God's Kingdom?

5. How do the ways you experience emotions affect what activities you do and with which people you most frequently spend time, and what have been the consequences for your spiritual development and service for expanding and improving God's Kingdom?

6. How do your interests influence what activities you do and with whom you most frequently come into contact, and what have been the consequences for your spiritual development and service to God's Kingdom?

7. How has your relationship with God influenced what activities you do and with which people you most frequently interact, and what have been the consequences for your spiritual development and your effectiveness for expanding and improving God's Kingdom?

Week Two Memory Verse

"… [L]ay up for yourselves treasures in heaven …." (Matthew 6:20, NKJV)

Week Two: Days Five and Six

Chose and Memorize a Life Verse

"Therefore you shall be perfect, just as your Father in heaven is perfect."

— Matthew 5:48 (NKJV)

What is a life verse? Many people discover a part of the Bible that encompasses some extremely important lesson that should never be far from their thoughts. After such a discovery, memorizing such a verse should be relatively easy because the lesson is so spiritually valuable and relevant to a believer's life.

Matthew 5:48 (NKJV) reminds us that although we have all sinned and need to repent and ask God for forgiveness, we are also capable of acting in perfect ways that bring God glory, draw us closer to Him, and expand and improve His Kingdom. You can use this lesson to find a verse that helps bring you closer to the perfection that God intends for you.

As you perceive God more fully, your relationship with Him becomes closer, and you develop spiritually, your life verse could possibly change. However, by responding *now* to His Word by concentrating on one verse, you will be gaining immediately applicable directions and encouragement that will further your spiritual development, time and again, in the meantime.

Many believers have shared their life verses with me. I have been fascinated to note that no two of them have selected the same verse. This variation is yet more evidence of the uniqueness that God has created in each of us.

Life verses can be inspired in so many ways that this lesson cannot begin to touch on them all. Let me mention a few possible sources of inspiration that could help start your thinking about what to focus on in His Word. For example, you might have had some remarkable experience that revealed God to you in more ways than at any other time. If that were the case, you might select a verse that resonates strongly with what you felt on that occasion. As a different example, you might be tempted to sin in a way that is very difficult for you to resist. To do better, you might look for a verse that would strengthen your resistance. Alternatively, a certain verse might be powerful for inspiring you to do God's will much more frequently in some particular aspect of your life. If changing your focus in such a way would make you act more fruitfully, such a verse could be a perfect choice. Or, if you want to become more loving with other people, a verse about how Jesus acted in such a way might encourage you to do so as well.

My testimony in Appendix B contains my life verse. If you read that testimony, I think you will understand why I chose it. Perhaps this example will help you search for a life verse if you don't already have one.

Experience God More Fully by Choosing and Memorizing a Life Verse

Many people already have life verses. You might find it helpful to ask other believers if they have chosen such a verse, what it is, and how the verse has affected their lives. You can probably find online materials where such topics are addressed, as well.

If you haven't yet thought about this subject, you might find it helpful to search for words in the Bible related to topics that strongly attract your attention and interest … or even where you would like to change. Following are some questions that may help your search:

1. What is the most valuable spiritual benefit that a life verse could bring to you for either drawing closer to God or for increasing and improving His Kingdom?

2. What are at least 10 moving and relevant verses that you might select? If you have access to either a searchable Website that contains Bible translations or to an indexed Bible translation, look for verses that address the relevant topics for you.

3. How might each of these possible life verses affect your spiritual sensitivities and actions?

4. What thoughts are most prominent in your mind after praying for guidance in selecting one of these verses?

5. What verse did you choose?

6. How will you memorize, remind yourself to meditate on, and act based on the point of this verse?

Week Two Memory Verse

"… [L]ay up for yourselves treasures in heaven …." (Matthew 6:20, NKJV)

Week Three: Days One and Two

Review How You Have Been Affected by Jesus Being Your Lord and Savior

"Come to Me, all you *who labor and are heavy laden,*
and I will give you rest.
Take My yoke upon you and learn from Me,
for I am gentle and lowly in heart,
and you will find rest for your souls.
For My yoke is *easy and My burden is light."*

— Matthew 11:28-30 (NKJV)

Learning that God wants us to serve His purposes for the Kingdom and to live a righteous life often strikes new believers as adding heavy burdens that make life more difficult. How can they possibly go from being "me" centered to becoming God centered and still deal with everything that already has them pretty fully occupied?

First, realize that you were filled with the Holy Spirit after accepting Jesus as your Lord and Savior. Acts 1:8 (NKJV) describes the consequences for the first believers by repeating Jesus' promise in His own words: "But you shall receive power when the Holy Spirit has come upon you; and you shall be witnesses to Me in Jerusalem, and in all Judea and Samaria, and to the end of the earth." Once the Holy Spirit is inside you, a transformation begins through this power to make you more like Jesus. You can also pray daily to be refilled with the Holy Spirit so that more of that power will be present and more transformation will occur. In addition, you will be able to draw on that Godly power when you serve the Kingdom. Further, God will direct you to ways of accomplishing more and more often doing the right thing.

Some people have compared the task of following Jesus to being like carrying one side of a very heavy burden with a partner who, while capable of lifting the whole load, wants us to participate to the full extent that we can. As a result, our share of the lifting is always well within the limits of our strength and endurance. As a believer, you may have already done things that created amazing results for the Kingdom, as compared with what you could have accomplished before accepting Jesus as your Lord and Savior.

A relationship can also be likened to a house or a building, in that the firmness and depth of the foundation determine how many upper floors can be added. In this lesson, we focus on your experiences in following Jesus that have firmed and deepened your relationship with Him to help you serve the Kingdom more effectively and often. As you reflect on these experiences, you will then be able to perceive more ways to draw closer to Him and to more strongly desire to do so.

Experience God More Fully by Remembering and Reviewing How Jesus Christ Being Your Lord and Savior Has Affected You

In some dimensions, your recollections of these effects might be incomplete. If you have access to people who knew you before, during, and after your acceptance of the free gift of Salvation, you may find it very enlightening to hear what they recall in these regards. Here are questions that you can use to examine yourself about the effects of accepting Salvation:

1. Since becoming a follower of Jesus, how have you become more righteous?

2. How have you become better able to serve God's Kingdom?

3. How have you become able to more effectively handle difficulties?

4. What burdens now seem lighter?

5. What worries have disappeared?

6. What blessings have you received for the first time?

7. What good works do you perform now that you didn't do before?

8. How do family and friends see you as being different?

9. What other changes have you noticed?

10. How do you feel about these changes?

11. How do you think God views these changes?

12. What new thing can you do today to expand or improve God's Kingdom that you could not have acted on before?

13. When will you start doing that new thing?

14. How did it feel to do that new thing?

Week Three Memory Verse

" … My yoke *is* easy and My burden is light." (Matthew 11:30, NKJV)

Week Three: Days Three and Four

Notice How God Attracts Your Attention

"For there is nothing hidden which will not be revealed,
nor has anything been kept secret but that it should come to light.
If anyone has ears to hear, let him hear."

Then He said to them, "Take heed what you hear.
With the same measure you use, it will be measured to you;
and to you who hear, more will be given.
For whoever has, to him more will be given;
but whoever does not have,
even what he has will be taken away from him."

— Mark 4:22-25 (NKJV)

Mark 4:22-25 (NKJV) indicates that what we need to know will be revealed. In addition, we will be rewarded for paying attention to what God wants us to know by subsequently having more revealed, enabling still more learning to occur. Conversely, if we do not pay attention, what we know will eventually be forgotten.

Have you ever picked up the Bible to look at a verse or a parable and unexpectedly found your eyes focused, instead, on a verse on the first page you "inadvertently" opened? If so, that's just one of the many ways that God could choose to send you a message. Prior to opening that Bible, you might have had an "irresistible" urge to look up what you originally intended to study. That urge can represent one of the many powerful ways that God gains your attention prior to delivering an important message He doesn't want you to miss.

If you haven't yet had either of those experiences, perhaps you've suddenly had a new and expanded understanding of some detail, verse, parable, or lesson while reading your Bible. Think back to how you came to be looking at the Bible then. The impetus to read might have come from God directing your attention.

Feelings of discomfort can work in a similar way. For instance, have you ever felt very uncomfortable in a certain place, so uncomfortable that you immediately left it? Such a feeling might have indicated that God wanted you to be elsewhere, either because of some problem with where you were or to accomplish some purpose of His that could only be done in a different place.

Difficulties can play a comparable role. You might have planned to take a family member to a certain restaurant that did not accept reservations. On arriving, you might have found that the wait would be very long. Due to that circumstance, you went elsewhere to eat. At the other restaurant, you might then have bumped into some friends with whom you had a good discussion about God. In such an instance, God might have attracted all of those other diners to the first restaurant just to divert you to where He wanted you to be, when He wanted you to be there, so you would have that discussion.

A conversation with others can also be a way that God gains your attention. The person speaking may have had one purpose in mind for selecting what was said, and yet God could cause you to perceive a totally different meaning that reveals Him and His purposes in some very fundamental and important ways.

His creatures can be another way He attracts your attention. He might send some beautiful birds to make you stop and admire His creation. While you were viewing this lovely sight, He might speak to you through the Holy Spirit about these birds in some way that would bring you closer to Him.

Some people also experience dreams, visions, or supernatural occurrences that redirect their attention in powerful and memorable ways to God's purposes. Sometimes the messages might be quite clear. Other times there might be symbols involved. Should any dream, vision, or supernatural occurrence happen and you feel there's an important message, pray for God to reveal more of His meaning to you.

Because of the unique way that God created you, His most effective ways of gaining your attention may have little or no effect on someone else. One of the benefits of being more conscious of how God has drawn your attention is to notice more often when He is about to reveal something to you.

Experience God More Fully by Noticing How He Attracts Your Attention

If relatively few ideas occur to you for addressing this subject, feel free to start noting whenever God succeeds in attracting your attention. I'm sure that within a few days or weeks you will be noticing more than ever before. Also, ask other believers how God attracts their attention. He may be trying to do the same with you! While no list of ways that God might have drawn your attention can hope to be complete, please use answering these questions to help you more often notice what He has been and is doing:

1. How has God used "accidents" to help you notice something that contributed to your spiritual development, your relationship with Him, or your service for His Kingdom?

2. How has God used your urges to direct you to something He wanted you to notice?

3. How has discomfort drawn your attention to what God intended?

4. How have the meanings of written words and symbols changed for you in ways that served God's purposes?

5. How has God used difficulties to put you in the right place at the right time?

6. How have words spoken or written by others caused your attention to shift to His different meaning for you?

7. What role has observing nature played in attracting your attention to His purposes?

8. How has God used visions, dreams, and spiritual experiences to direct you down His righteous paths?

9. In what other ways has God drawn your attention?

10. How else would you like for God to capture your awareness?

11. What signs of His messages should you look for daily?

12. Do you see any of such signs now?

13. How do you feel when you receive an indication that He wants your attention?

14. What do you do then?

15. Would you like to respond differently?

Week Three Memory Verse

" … My yoke *is* easy and My burden is light." (Matthew 11:30, NKJV)

Week Three: Days Five and Six

Visit Where You Most Feel God's Presence

"Abide in Me, and I in you.
As the branch cannot bear fruit of itself,
unless it abides in the vine,
neither can you, unless you abide in Me.
I am the vine, you are *the branches.*
He who abides in Me, and I in him, bears much fruit;
for without Me you can do nothing.
If anyone does not abide in Me,
he is cast out as a branch and is withered;
and they gather them and throw them *into the fire,*
and they are burned.
If you abide in Me, and My words abide in you,
you will ask what you desire,
and it shall be done for you.
By this My Father is glorified,
that you bear much fruit;
so you will be My disciples."

— John 15:4-8 (NKJV)

In John 15:4-8 (NKJV), Jesus reminds us that our connection to Him must be continual and strong. One possible way to increase and maintain that connection is by spending more time where we most strongly feel His presence.

Each of us associates certain places with God more than some other places. For example, few would find a gasoline filling station to be as spiritual as a church sanctuary. However, if God had appeared to you in a vision at the filling station, you could rightly feel His strong presence there whenever you returned and recalled that experience.

The example of Jesus is instructive for such purposes. He spent time with His Father by withdrawing to where He could pray quietly, such as at the Garden of Gethsemane (Matthew 26:36, NKJV).

In addition, in describing the Lord's Prayer to His disciples, Jesus indicated that the location for prayer was important: "But you, when you pray, go into your room, and when you have shut your door, pray to your Father who *is* in the secret *place;* and your Father who sees in secret will reward you openly." (Matthew 6:6, NKJV) If you have often followed that advice by using a private place for your daily devotions, you may well sense God's presence more strongly there than in many other locations.

As we explored during the lesson on days one and two of week one, there are views of and places in God's creation that can cause us to feel His presence more strongly, as well. As you think about places in nature where you have gained some spiritual insight that has stayed with you, such a locale may have contributed to some of what you experienced.

Of course, timing may strongly influence when and where you feel God's presence. A place where you go for powerfully moving Easter sunrise services might not provide the same experience when visited alone at noon in winter.

Experience God More Fully by Visiting Where You Most Feel His Presence

While it's good to remember where and when you most feel God's presence, it's more fruitful to experience more of God's presence by actually going to such places at the best times. During this lesson, you should visit as many of these locations as you can at the optimal moments. However, don't stop doing so after these two days. Visit such locations as often as you can. And be open to discovering more of such places. Pray for the Holy Spirit to lead you in both such ways. Here are some questions to help you focus your visitations:

1. Where have you strongly felt God's presence?

2. Which of these places are where you can visit them during the next two days and potentially have a somewhat similar reaction?

3. Where else that you haven't visited might provide a strong sense of Him?

4. How can you arrange to visit all of such places more often?

5. What will be most important for you to do while at each one?

6. What insights did you gain from these visits during these two days?

7. What role should such visits play in your future?

Week Three Memory Verse

" … My yoke *is* easy and My burden is light." (Matthew 11:30, NKJV)

Week Four: Days One and Two

Think about and Learn from Those Who Are Most like Jesus

"And He will set the sheep on His right hand,
but the goats on the left.
Then the King will say to those on His right hand,
'Come, you blessed of My Father, inherit the kingdom
prepared for you from the foundation of the world:
for I was hungry and you gave Me food;
I was thirsty and you gave Me drink;
I was a stranger and you took Me in;
I was naked and you clothed Me;
I was sick and you visited Me;
I was in prison and you came to Me.'"

— Matthew 25:33-36 (NKJV)

Jesus made it clear that we are to be active in sharing the Gospel with nonbelievers, teaching believers to become disciples (Matthew 28:19-20, NKJV), and providing for those who most need our assistance (Matthew 25:33-36, NKJV, for believers, and Luke 10:25-37, NKJV, for all others). By being quite aware of how much greater Jesus, the Son of God, is than we are, it's easy to think of what He asks us to do as being beyond what we can accomplish.

However, if we carefully note exactly what Jesus commanded and taught in these verses, we can see that the demands are not as great as they might seem at first. In terms of the Great Commission (Matthew 28:19-20, NKJV), we should appreciate that until people know the Gospel, they aren't going to gain Salvation. Clearly, the Good News that the Gospel brought to us in gaining Salvation should be something we would then want to joyfully share with others. For those who are new believers, great hunger and thirst for Godly knowledge are common. If we simply show up and try to help such a new believer, we should be able to help her or him become more fruitful as a disciple.

In Matthew 25:33-36 (NKJV) and Luke 10:25-37 (NKJV), we can see that we aren't expected to provide someone every meal for the rest of his or her life. Instead, we are to feed someone when she or he is hungry, or cannot take care of him- or herself. Why wouldn't we do that? I find it hard to imagine that anyone who wasn't also dying of thirst and had some healthy liquid to share wouldn't provide it to a thirsty person. If, for example, we see someone who is new and looking a little befuddled enter our church, why wouldn't we give some directions, provide a meal, and possibly extend some ongoing hospitality? Anyone who is naked clearly needs clothes. Few would be unwilling to provide such coverings. While most of us aren't physicians or nurses, we can clearly visit someone who is ill and provide whatever support and comfort our company, words, and prayers can bring. Those in prison cannot leave, so we need to visit them before we can help them in whatever ways God wants. In sum, the tasks mentioned in Matthew 25:33-36 (NKJV) aren't all that demanding, except that we must be prepared to put someone else's needs ahead of our own desires in the particular moment. Doing so is good for us when the result is to become less selfish. Although the Parable of the Good Samaritan (Luke 10:25-37, NKJV) clearly describes greater burdens in providing help, those burdens are simply commensurate with the substantial needs of the naked, half-dead traveler in the parable who had been robbed.

If you ask most believers, they will indicate that they haven't yet done all the things that Matthew 25:33-36 (NKJV) includes. If encouraged to do so, some people would probably say that they probably won't ever do at least a few of such things, perhaps such as not visiting anyone in prison.

Yet when He said these things, Jesus knew that all of these actions are good *for us*, as well as for those who are the obvious beneficiaries. How can we come to fully appreciate this perspective? In many cases, finding those who happily and enthusiastically perform each of such activities can help us to notice the benefits for us in God's plan of service.

Rather than seeking a remarkable person who might overwhelm us with her or his righteousness in looking for such information, we can potentially learn more by speaking with a number of seemingly ordinary believers who are engaged in such activities. If we ask these people to tell us about the experience of serving in these ways, we are likely to hear about activities we can imagine doing, ones that can help us develop Godly desires to do likewise. In time, our fruitfulness will then grow after we follow Jesus' guidance and the experiences of others in these regards.

Experience God More Fully by Thinking about and Learning from Those Who Are Most like Jesus

Chances are that you haven't thought much about this topic. You may need to schedule some additional quiet time to think about who can serve as a source for your learning. Pray for God's directions through gaining the help of the Holy Spirit. Acting on this lesson will clearly take you longer than two days, so keep at it! Hopefully, the following questions will help you focus your attention as you do:

1. Who are some ordinary believers joyfully and actively sharing the Gospel, helping believers to become better disciples of Jesus, feeding the hungry, providing for the thirsty, taking in strangers, clothing those who need garments, and visiting the sick and those who are incarcerated?

2. Who else can you add to the list of those you know, or have heard of or read about?

3. How can you learn more from as many of these believers as possible about why they do what they do, how they do it, and what the effects have been on their lives?

4. How can you get help in learning how to experience the same effects?

5. How can you perform each activity before this course ends?

6. Who can you speak with today or tomorrow to begin your learning?

7. Can someone who is already doing so join with you during the first time you serve in one of these ways?

8. What temptations do you need to overcome to enable you to complete such learning and begin to apply it?

9. How can you be faithful in continually applying what you learn?

Week Four Memory Verse

" … [L]ove your enemies, bless those who curse you, do good to those who hate you, and pray for those who spitefully use you and persecute you, that you may be sons of your Father in heaven …." (Matthew 5:44-45, NKJV)

Week Four: Days Three and Four

Forgive Others

"For if you forgive men their trespasses,
your heavenly Father will also forgive you.
But if you do not forgive men their trespasses,
neither will your Father forgive your trespasses."

— Matthew 6:14-15 (NKJV)

Many believers find themselves unable to forgive some of the wrongs done to them by other people, even though Jesus explained in Matthew 6:14-15 (NKJV) that we must do so to gain forgiveness from God. In other places, such as Luke 10:27 (NKJV), Jesus told us that we are to love our neighbors as ourselves. In doing so, there's no indication that our neighbors have to be loveable to qualify. Jesus also said in part of Matthew 5:44 (NKJV) that we are to love our enemies. When we think about forgiving enemies, our challenge is significant: We must forgive a nearby enemy so completely that we can then love and act lovingly to the person we have forgiven!

Matthew 6:14-15 (NKJV) provides a substantial clue as to how we can become so forgiving: God's love for us is so great that He sent His only Son to take the punishment that we deserve for our sins to redeem us from them. When God has been and is so good to us, how can we want to do any less for those who have harmed us?

For some believers, even appreciating God's grace isn't enough to enable them to forgive deep hurts. For example, I often hear people tell about feuding with some family member, sometimes for decades. In some of such cases, the unforgiving believer is waiting for the other person to take the first step for reconciliation. Where does the Bible say that we should only forgive those who ask forgiveness? No, Matthew 6:14-15 (NKJV) makes it clear that we are to forgive everyone!

Let me suggest a practical reason why Jesus told us to forgive everyone: *Doing so is good for us.* Here's what I mean. If you haven't forgiven someone, then every time you think of that event or that person the pain of the experience recurs. As an analogy, when such a recollection happens, it's almost as if you have just thrust a knife into a wound that hasn't yet healed. By contrast, when we forgive, the pain of the occurrence is ultimately eliminated. Then the wound heals. We don't keep re-experiencing what had happened. Our lives can then contain more peace and calm. Isn't that what Jesus wants for us?

Another reason to forgive is remembering how good it felt to be forgiven by others and by God. In many cases (especially where the misdeed was a very great one with significant, ongoing harm), being forgiven can feel like having a two-ton weight lifted from your chest. Imagine the joy you could feel by sometimes providing such relief for someone else!

In addition, we should remember that we are going to do wrong things in the future, despite our best intentions not to do so. Wouldn't we want to be forgiven, both by God and those we have harmed?

With our own strength, we may not be able to forgive an enemy … or even an unrepentant family member. As the Holy Spirit transforms us into being more like Jesus, we can receive healing from the spiritual effects of the injury so that we can forgive the person who inflicted it and move on. Pray daily for the Lord to transform you in this way until you have forgiven all your enemies … as well as all others who have trespassed against you to any degree. Learn thereafter to forgive quickly and completely.

Experience God More Fully by Forgiving Others

Forgiving others, especially those who annoy or anger you the most, isn't something you are likely to learn how to do in just two days. So with this lesson, your most important task is addressing daily from now on how to do so with God's help. The following questions are designed for you to ask daily for helping you make the transformation that Jesus wants you to undergo:

1. Whom have you not forgiven?

2. Why have you not forgiven these people?

3. Have you asked God for His help in forgiving them?

4. Do you make forgiving people part of your daily prayers, before you ask God to forgive you for your sins?

5. Are you confessing to God when you don't forgive?

6. Whom will you forgive now, for the first time?

7. How does it feel to forgive someone you haven't forgiven before?

8. How can you remain focused on these questions each day?

Week Four Memory Verse

" … [L]ove your enemies, bless those who curse you, do good to those who hate you, and pray for those who spitefully use you and persecute you, that you may be sons of your Father in heaven …." (Matthew 5:44-45, NKJV)

Week Four: Days Five and Six

Repent, Ask Forgiveness, and Feel Forgiven

"Judge not, and you shall not be judged.
Condemn not, and you shall not be condemned.
Forgive, and you will be forgiven."

— Luke 6:37 (NKJV)

The verses of Luke 24:46-47 (NKJV) add to Luke 6:37 (NKJV) the following observations about gaining forgiveness from God: "Thus it is written, and thus it was necessary for the Christ to suffer and to rise from the dead the third day, and that repentance and remission of sins should be preached in His name to all nations, beginning at Jerusalem." As believers in Jesus, we need to turn away (repent) from sins, request God's help to not sin again, humbly ask for His forgiveness, and then receive and act on that forgiveness.

As the prior lesson pointed out, one of the sins that some believers need to repent and request forgiveness for is *not forgiving others*. If that's your circumstance, be sure to repent now. Of course, if you have other sins you have not yet repented and asked God to forgive, be sure to address those sins now with God, as well.

Let's consider repentance. Our reason for repenting sins shouldn't be based on having been caught or embarrassed. Our repentance should, instead, be founded in our love of God and our desire to live the full life that He has planned for us. Sin distances us from Him, as well as interferes with His plans for our fruitful lives. The act of repenting should also bring awareness of our relationship with God to the fore: He's our Creator and Heavenly Father who loves us and wants what is good for us.

How often should we repent committing a sin? Some people are confused on this point. You only need to do so once for each commission because Jesus' sacrifice on the cross wiped away the consequences of sin for those who believe in Him and repent. However, if you repeat the sin, you need to repent and ask for forgiveness again after the repetition occurs. To do better in this regard, after glorifying God in your prayers, ask the Holy Spirit to help you completely notice your unrepented sins, so that you can repent each one before then asking for forgiveness.

Some people report not feeling forgiven after repenting and asking for forgiveness. It's possible that some of these people may not have been forgiven. For example, if you intend to keep doing the same sin, you haven't repented and you won't be forgiven. Also, if you haven't forgiven others for harming you, God won't forgive you. In other cases, you just may not have confidence in God's promises in this regard. If you don't feel forgiven and aren't sure what's missing, ask God to show you so that you can make amends and receive His wonderful and blessed forgiveness.

Believers describe God's forgiveness in different ways. Because you are unique and valuable in His eyes, feel comfortable realizing that your experiences with being forgiven by Him may be quite different from those of another believer you know. Signs of being forgiven will often include feeling more humble, due to becoming more aware of how weak one is in resisting temptation and also to having greater appreciation for God's great power in providing forgiveness. Relief can also be experienced, particularly when the sin will have ongoing consequences for you and others. Although the consequences of such sin cannot or will not be undone in many cases, at least you can once again feel that you are a loved child of the Great Father and be a friend and sister or brother of the Lord Jesus Christ. You may also feel a strong desire to do better in the future, as well as be encouraged to look for ways to escape from temptation when it presents itself. The Holy Spirit may provide you with guidance for how to accomplish such a desirable result. Lastly, your life should feel lighter and more peaceful.

As you experience some of these or other positive feelings, realize what a great gift God has given us in being able to forgive others. Think what a great blessing awareness of our forgiveness confers on them! Give this gift as often as possible. Make the questions in the next section ones that you ask daily.

Experience God More Fully by Repenting, Asking Forgiveness, and Feeling Forgiven

These questions are designed to give you a way to focus your spirit and attention so that your life will be more completely filled with forgiveness, both received and given:

1. What sins have you not yet repented?

2. Have you asked the Holy Spirit today to help you identify any other sins you haven't repented?

3. Have you asked the Holy Spirit today to help you avoid such sins in the future?

4. Have you asked God to forgive you of all sins that you have committed and repented?

5. Do you feel forgiven?

6. If you don't feel forgiven, what is it about your relationship with God that might be blocking either feeling or actually being forgiven?

7. If you aren't forgiven, what do you need to do to gain His forgiveness?

8. Who could you forgive now for the first time in a way that would lighten that person's life?

9. How does it feel to have forgiven someone in this way?

Week Four Memory Verse

" … [L]ove your enemies, bless those who curse you, do good to those who hate you, and pray for those who spitefully use you and persecute you, that you may be sons of your Father in heaven …." (Matthew 5:44-45, NKJV)

Week Five: Days One and Two

Spend Increased Time with, Pay Greater Attention to, and Learn More about Our Heavenly Father, His Son Jesus, and the Holy Spirit

"As the Father loved Me,
I also have loved you;
abide in My love.
If you keep My commandments,
you will abide in My love,
just as I have kept My Father's commandments
and abide in His love.
These things I have spoken to you,
that My joy may remain in you, and
that your joy may be full."

— John 15:9-10 (NKJV)

Isn't it wonderful that Jesus wants us to feel His love so much that His joy will continually fill us? While the two verses above correctly point to the benefits of keeping Jesus' commandments, doing so will be much easier after you spend increased time with, pay greater attention to, and learn more about Our Heavenly Father, the Lord Jesus, and the Holy Spirit, our subject for this lesson.

In Part Three, we will be looking closely at a number of practices that can help you to abide more fully in Jesus' love. In this lesson, we focus on just one of those practices: spending more of your day thinking about and being in touch with our Heavenly Father, the Lord Jesus Christ, and the Holy Spirit.

Sermons often encourage keeping God and His commands in mind throughout the week, rather than just thinking about Him when you are in church. Most people will nod their heads in agreement during such sermons, but many of these same people will lack a plan for how to do so once they leave the sanctuary.

Since God has called each of us to participate differently in the Kingdom, each person's plan for being in a relationship with and serving Him undoubtedly diverges from that of any other believer. However, some plan elements are more likely to be included for each one of us. This lesson briefly introduces you to two of such elements and encourages you to experience each one more often, beginning today and tomorrow.

Perhaps the most common element is to spend daily uninterrupted time with God. It doesn't matter when you do so, but such an opportunity to think about, listen to, and speak with God can make a huge difference in how you spend the rest of your day. For many people, such a quiet time includes praising God for His amazing goodness, thanking Him for all He has done, studying the Bible, thinking about how to apply what was learned from Bible study, repenting sins, asking forgiveness, requesting to be refilled with the Holy Spirit, and making notes on what has been learned about and experienced with God.

However, we shouldn't limit our daily time with God to just one occasion. You can also draw closer by looking and listening for more communications *from* Him, whether while considering a different Bible verse, hearing worship music, thinking about what other believers say and do, evaluating the situations we encounter, observing the natural world around us, praying, or meditating on the apparent meaning of any supernatural experiences we have.

Naturally, we can also increase our communications *to* Him through prayer (such as by asking for guidance, strength, and provision to do His will) when faced with something challenging. Such prayers don't have to be long or only occur once daily. Instead, we should pray whenever we want or need to say something to Him, even if we don't have a particular purpose in mind when we begin.

While we perform acts that could expand or improve His Kingdom, we should also keep Him in the front of our minds. Before and while so acting, we can also ask for guidance in how to be more fruitful.

When there are things we don't understand about God, especially when our faith feels weak, we should study to learn more, both on our own and by seeking aid from those with greater knowledge. We will be exploring some qualities of Our Heavenly Father, His Son Jesus, and the Holy Spirit during the first week of Part Three. Please note that there are many pastors who have put individual lessons online that discuss every chapter in the Bible. You can listen to such resources to help expand your understanding of something that is confusing or unclear. In all cases, keep asking God to teach you what you don't yet understand.

Finally, remind yourself several times a day to spend more time with, pay attention to, and learn about Our Heavenly Father, His Son Jesus, and the Holy Spirit.

Experience God More Fully by Spending More Time with, Paying Attention to, and Learning about Our Heavenly Father, the Lord Jesus Christ, and the Holy Spirit

To go from having a desire to draw closer to God and to actually doing so requires intention and action. In this section of the lesson, you will find questions that should assist you in adding more helpful actions to your good intentions in this regard:

1. Do you spend uninterrupted time daily with God?

2. If you do not, when would be a good time and place each day to do so?

3. If you already do so, could you increase the time?

4. If yes, what activities does God call you to engage in then?

5. What do you need to learn about God?

6. Where can you gain such information?

7. How should you abide in God more completely throughout each day?

8. How can you be reminded throughout the day to spend more time with and learning about Him?

Week Five Memory Verse

"If you keep My commandments, you will abide in My love …." (John 15:10, NKJV)

Week Five: Days Three and Four

Feel God's Love More Fully

"He who has My commandments and keeps them,
it is he who loves Me.
And he who loves Me will be loved by My Father,
and I will love him and manifest Myself to him."

— John 14:21 (NKJV)

As John 14:21 (NKJV) reminds us, knowing and keeping Jesus' commandments show our love for Him and attract the Father's love to us, as well. You have probably had a somewhat similar experience as a child. At least sometimes, you probably obeyed what the adults you loved asked you to do, simply because of your love for them, regardless of whether you understood the purposes of the requests.

What may be somewhat less clear is how knowing and keeping such commandments can cause you to more fully feel God's love. Let's look more closely at this phenomenon.

Imagine simply being relieved of guilt caused by having done something wrong. Most people carry a heavy burden of guilt due to having realized their errors and having seen bad consequences until God and other people have forgiven them. If you avoid committing such sins, then you are going to have a more pleasant life.

In week one, we considered God's creation, the ways He has blessed you, and the prayer requests that He has fulfilled. If you take time to reflect on these dimensions of your relationship with Him, you have to feel His love to a greater degree … especially if you can add insights in these regards gained through these lessons to what you had previously noticed.

In week three, you thought about how Jesus being your Lord and Savior has affected you and how God has attracted your attention. Daily reflection on those specific blessings will also increase your awareness of God's love for you. Also in week three, you visited at least one place where you strongly feel God's presence at certain times. Think, too, daily about the loving gift that God has given you by providing such places.

In week four, you learned to be diligent in forgiving others and receiving forgiveness from God. Bathe in the loving kindness of that wonderful help from Him.

In the prior lesson, you concentrated on spending more time with and learning about God. As you made such changes, I'm sure you felt more of God's presence … and His love.

God wants you to have a life centered on your relationship with Him, a relationship founded in His everlasting, perfect love. Has anyone else come close to loving you so much? Even if you have had such good fortune from the love of another person, such as a parent or spouse, keep in mind that it was God's plan to create that loving relationship for you with the other person.

Finally, recall that God intends for you to have eternal life with Him after leaving Earth, without experiencing any tears, pain, or sorrow there with Him. So claim that promise with every fiber of your being to enter into the love that underlies His wonderful plan.

Experience God More Fully by Feeling His Love More Completely

As limited beings, it's easy for us to be blind, deaf, and unfeeling in noticing and appreciating some aspects of the love that God has for us. For instance, Our Heavenly Father sometimes disciplines us, as any good parent would, for our own good because He loves us. At the time we receive such discipline, we may not interpret that experience as an expression of love. With increased time and attention, we can gradually appreciate more of His love. You'll need to stay focused in this way after you leave this lesson. Use the following questions to begin expanding your ability to feel God's love:

1. How many of the numerous ways that God loves you do you feel at any one time?

2. Does what causes you to feel God's love also connect you to other reasons for feeling His love?

3. How can you combine more ways of simultaneously feeling His love?

4. What reminders of His love would cause you to feel more loved at all times?

5. How can you increase your focus on such reminders?

6. What daily experiences can cause you to feel His love more fully?

7. How can you be sure to have such daily experiences?

8. Which of those experiences can you have now?

9. How did your ability to feel God's love change as you engaged with the first fourteen lessons in *Disciple*?

Week Five Memory Verse

"If you keep My commandments, you will abide in My love …." (John 15:10, NKJV)

Week Five: Days Five and Six

Know Peace

"Let not your heart be troubled;
you believe in God, believe also in Me.

"In My Father's house are many mansions;
if it were not so, I would have told you.
I go to prepare a place for you.
And if I go and prepare a place for you,
I will come again and receive you to Myself;
that where I am, there you may be also.

"And where I go you know, and the way you know."

Thomas said to Him, "Lord, we do not know
where You are going, and how can we know the way?"

Jesus said to him, "I am the way, the truth, and the life.
No one comes to the Father except through Me."

— John 14:1-6 (NKJV)

When you experience God more fully, you can eventually be able to always feel His presence and peace. As the disciples found during the tempest on the Sea of Galilee, Jesus can calm a life-threatening storm. You just need to call on Him, and you have access to the Father and all of the power in the universe.

Keep in mind that God knows what's coming. In fact, He sent Jesus to pay the price for your sins so that you could have a full and forgiven life with Him for all eternity. Jesus has already gone ahead to prepare a place for you in that eternity.

So when you feel any despair, remember that whatever upsets you is no surprise to God. And He can handle whatever it is so that your calling for serving Him can be accomplished.

While we will have trials in this life, we should remember that He is there with us, as Psalm 23 (NKJV) tells us so eloquently:

The LORD *is* my shepherd;
I shall not want.
He makes me to lie down in green pastures;
He leads me beside the still waters.
He restores my soul;

He leads me in the paths of righteousness
For His name's sake.
Yea, though I walk through the valley of the shadow of death,
I will fear no evil;
For You *are* with me;
Your rod and Your staff, they comfort me.

You prepare a table before me in the presence of my enemies;
You anoint my head with oil;
My cup runs over.
Surely goodness and mercy shall follow me
All the days of my life; And I will dwell in the house of the LORD
Forever.

Experience God More Fully by Knowing His Peace

While almost everyone will tell you that they need and want more peace in their lives, many of those same people have no idea for how to find and retain greater peace. The following questions are provided to make the connection to peace easier to accomplish, as well as longer lasting:

1. How has God protected you in dangerous circumstances?

2. Do you now feel the peace that such protection then brought you?

3. What promises made by the Father or the Lord Jesus Christ make you feel the most peaceful?

4. Would it help you to feel more peaceful if you memorized those promises and repeated them daily?

5. What else can you do now, and every day, to more fully know His peace and rest more completely in it?

6. How did it feel to do those things?

Week Five Memory Verse

"If you keep My commandments, you will abide in My love …." (John 15:10, NKJV)

I pray that these first fifteen lessons have enabled you to experience God more fully and to rely more on His goodness in all aspects of your life. Don't stop now. Keep experiencing and relying on Him more every day as reliable paths to drawing closer to Him!

Part Two:

Live the Gospel

God, who made the world and everything in it,
since He is Lord of heaven and earth,
does not dwell in temples made with hands.
Nor is He worshiped with men's hands,
as though He needed anything,
since He gives to all life, breath, and all things.

And He has made from one blood every nation of men
to dwell on all the face of the earth, and has determined
their preappointed times and
the boundaries of their dwellings,
so that they should seek the Lord, in the hope
that they might grope for Him and find Him,
though He is not far from each one of us;
for in Him we live and move and have our being,
as also some of your own poets have said,
"For we are also His offspring."

Therefore, since we are the offspring of God,
we ought not to think that the Divine Nature
is like gold or silver or stone,
something shaped by art and man's devising.

Truly, these times of ignorance God overlooked, but
now commands all men everywhere to repent,
because He has appointed a day
on which He will judge the world
in righteousness by the Man whom He has ordained.
He has given assurance of this to all
by raising Him from the dead.

— Acts 17:24-31 (NKJV)

The verses in Acts 17:24-31 (NKJV) capture how the Apostle Paul explained the Gospel to the idol-worshipping nonbelievers in Athens. Another good statement of the Gospel can be found in Peter's address to the people of Jerusalem on the day of Pentecost, as captured in Acts 2:14:39 (NKJV).

In Part Two, we will explore and experience how to live the Gospel more completely by following the most important commandments of Jesus. Our initial focus will be on how to love others, especially those we don't love now. When we love others as God loves us, our love will lead us to follow the commandments of Jesus more fully and thereby abide in His love, a subject we explored in days three and four of week five in Part One.

After that, we will engage in lessons about helping all people, including those we had formerly found it hard to love.

Through having the experiences in these lessons, your life will become much more like that which God planned for you. May He abundantly bless you as you continue to apply this part of *Disciple* for the rest of your life!

Week One: Days One and Two

See Others as Jesus Does

But Jesus said, "Let the little children come to Me,
and do not forbid them;
for of such is the kingdom of heaven."

— Matthew 19:14 (NKJV)

"Are not five sparrows sold for two copper coins?
And not one of them is forgotten before God.

"But the very hairs of your head are all numbered.
Do not fear therefore;
you are of more value than many sparrows."

— Luke 12:6-7 (NKJV)

And He stretched out His hand toward His disciples and said,
"Here are My mother and My brothers!
For whoever does the will of My Father in heaven is
My brother and sister and mother."

— Matthew 12:49-50 (NKJV)

While many more verses could be added to describe other dimensions of how Jesus sees others (including us), I believe that the verses above adequately exemplify the fundamental point: *Jesus has high regard for the potential in all people, saved and unsaved, and He treats us as family members when we follow God's will.* Take a minute to let that point sink deeply into your heart, soul, spirit, and mind.

By applying this lesson and the next five, you will experience turning His high regard for your potential and desire to have a spiritual relationship with you into your feeling more love for one and all. You will study and apply verses while doing so that will help build your appreciation for how Jesus sees others and shift your way of thinking closer to His.

Regarding people from Jesus' perspective won't at first feel natural (or very easy in some cases). One reason for having such difficulty is due to our being keen observers of how others are different from one another … and especially with regard to any differences from us. However, making such observations isn't the end of the story. Any noticing of differences can potentially lead us in one of three directions: a positive, a neutral, or a negative one.

If we focus on things about someone that make us appreciate him or her more, enable us to be in a closer relationship with her or him, and act in more loving ways, then the observations have led to a Godly, positive result. If, instead, we take no action based on what we observe that could build a loving relationship, then there has been neither a positive nor a negative consequence … except in the negative sense of having missed an opportunity to love and do something good. When we use any differences we have noted to make judgments about others that cause us to see them as "inferior," we will have usually placed an obstacle in the way of our potentially loving them, except perhaps through feeling pity. Permit a big enough obstacle of this sort to develop in our hearts and minds, and we will have sinned by not loving others as ourselves.

We should, instead, view any differences among people's unchangeable characteristics as merely signs of God's good plan at work in their lives, a plan that will provide more fruit for His Kingdom and bless them and others as they do His will. A helpful thought after noticing such differences is to contemplate how such characteristics might advance His plans. For instance, someone who has such poor eyesight that it cannot be corrected by human hands might someday be healed by faith, providing then a powerful, living testimony that God is active in the world. If such a healing did not occur, that same individual might, instead, focus more easily on spiritual realities than on what can be seen in the physical world.

Although Jesus is clearly our superior in every way we can imagine, He humbled Himself to endure a painful and humiliating death on the cross to save us, and He wants to be in a relationship with us. The Apostle Paul captured the significance of acting with a heart full of such Jesus-like humility with this instruction: "*Let* nothing *be done* through selfish ambition or conceit, but in lowliness of mind let each esteem others better than himself" (Philippians 2:3, NKJV). Keep that humble perspective in mind!

Live the Gospel by Seeing Others as Jesus Does

Transitioning to perceiving others as Jesus does can be a substantial and lengthy process. The following questions are designed to help you begin that transformation:

1. What differences in others cause you to judge them as inferior?

2. How might Jesus view the same differences as actually being advantages for increasing and improving God's Kingdom?

3. Are your judgments in such cases tied at all to feeling pride in some gift that God has given you?

4. If you feel any such pride, have you repented doing so, praised and thanked God for His gift, and asked Him to help you view the gift with proper humility?

5. What mental barriers and habits cause you to be ambitious or proud, rather than simply humble, while with others?

6. Have you asked God to remove those barriers and to help you change the habits?

7. Who can you see now afresh, as Jesus does, for the first time?

8. Who else can you see now from a humble perspective?

9. How can you act differently with each person, as a result?

10. How did it feel to do so?

11. How can you continue in learning to see others as Jesus does?

<u>Week One Memory Verse</u>

"For whoever does the will of My Father in heaven is My brother and sister and mother." (Matthew 12:50, NKJV)

Week One: Days Three and Four

Increase Your Love for Others

Jesus said to him,
"'You shall love the LORD your God with all your
heart, with all your soul, and with all your mind.'
This is the first and great commandment.
And the second is like it:
'You shall love your neighbor as yourself.'
On these two commandments hang all the Law and the Prophets."

— Matthew 22:37-40 (NKJV)

"A new commandment I give to you, that you love one another;
as I have loved you, that you also love one another.
By this all will know that you are My disciples,
if you have love for one another."

— John 13:34-35 (NKJV)

While many believers struggle with the idea that they should love others as much as they love themselves ... listed by Jesus as being just behind loving God fully in importance as a commandment ... they can easily miss the point of John 13:34-35 (NKJV): Our love for other believers should be as great as the love that Jesus has for us, an unlimited love that includes willingness to make any sacrifice that's good for the loved one. Think about this point for a moment. It's humbling to do so.

You obviously aren't going to develop such love without lots of help. Because you are filled with the Holy Spirit and you will abide in Christ's love if you follow His commandments, you can use those resources to provide the direction and strength you need to make an ideal transformation in how you view, consider, feel, and act with others.

Since we will be looking at several kinds of challenges in making such a transformation in the next few lessons in this part, this lesson just focuses on a few basic principles that can help lay a firm foundation for making such a transformation in terms of considering each person you encounter or think about. Here is the first transformational principle: *Notice everyone.*

Jesus provided plenty of examples in this regard. For instance, while on His way to raise a little girl from the dead (as described in Matthew 9:18-26, NKJV), a woman who had been bleeding for twelve years touched His clothing and was healed. Undoubtedly, many people were touching Him and His clothes at about the same time. Yet, Jesus noted that this healing had occurred and spoke to the woman, commenting that her faith had made her well. Consider, too, how in the Parable of the Good Samaritan (Luke 10:25-37, NKJV) the Samaritan's actions suggest that anyone within sight is to be treated as a neighbor who should be loved, even if doing so means violating some religious traditions and incurring considerable inconvenience and expense.

The usual tendency, in contrast, is to scan a group of people and note the most interesting, attractive, or similar ones. When we do that, we aren't really considering everyone with the love of Jesus. We need to take the time to consider each person individually and to think about how much Jesus loves this person as we consider her or him.

Here's the second principle: *Show God-like love for at least one of those you see who seems to need it the most.* After you have thought about each person in your vicinity from God's perspective, the Holy Spirit will help you identify those who most need your love. These may be people who look sad, or who are just being ignored by many of the other people in the vicinity, as was the half-dead victim in the Parable of the Good Samaritan. As an example, you might find that many people are looking over top of someone who is sitting in a wheelchair. You can, instead, make eye contact, smile, and start a conversation with that individual.

Live the Gospel by Increasing Your Love for Others

It's easy to consider love as being just another emotion among the many we experience. Filling your life with more love for others requires you to enable your love to dominate all your other emotions. You won't accomplish this result in two days. However, by answering and acting on what you learn from the following questions, you will begin to gain such ascendancy for love in your life:

1. What differences can cause you to feel less loving toward other people?

2. How would Jesus see those differences as being a blessing for the person in helping to expand and improve God's Kingdom?

3. How can you change how you think about others to be more like Jesus' perspective?

4. Who do you *not* normally notice in a group?

5. How can you be sure that you notice such people?

6. What signs of needing God's love will you look for in those you encounter?

7. What kinds of needs for God-like love will you supply?

8. Who can you act lovingly to today who doesn't expect it and will be greatly touched by receiving your loving attention?

9. How did it feel to do so?

10. How can you do so more often?

Week One Memory Verse

"For whoever does the will of My Father in heaven is My brother and sister and mother." (Matthew 12:50, NKJV)

Week One: Days Five and Six

Love More People

Then He also said to him who invited Him,
"When you give a dinner or a supper,
do not ask your friends, your brothers,
your relatives, nor rich neighbors,
lest they also invite you back, and you be repaid.
But when you give a feast, invite
the poor, the maimed, the lame, the blind.
And you will be blessed, because they cannot repay you;
for you shall be repaid at the resurrection of the just."

— Luke 14:12-14 (NKJV)

In Luke 14:12-14 (NKJV), Jesus gave a direction that must have surprised His host, a ruler of the Pharisees, who had invited Jesus to dine with him on the Sabbath. Notice the parallels to what Jesus said in Matthew 25:25-46 (NKJV) about how He will judge the nations in part by whom they have served.

While many parts of the Bible inspire many believers to take immediate action, Jesus' words in Luke 14:12-14 (NKJV) may not. Imagine someone planning a wedding reception. The expense is often enormous, the guest list has been added to many times so that no feelings will be hurt among relatives and friends, and those who are to be married, as well as those who are paying for the wedding, want everything to be perfect. I cannot recall anyone arranging such an event telling me that she or he wanted to also invite the poor, the maimed, the lame, and the blind to join the festivities.

Learning to love more people than you do now doesn't happen overnight. In fact, merely providing such a feast wouldn't be a loving thing to do if the motive was to gain future rewards from God. Before such openness in loving more people can occur, a change of heart has to take place.

The words of Jesus in these verses give us an indication of what can be a helpful first step: *Spend time being kind to people you don't normally get to know.* In the process, you may well find these individuals to be more interesting and lovable than you ever imagined. With a somewhat changed perception of such individuals, you will be more likely to seek out someone who is different from you the next time there is an opportunity to do so.

In addition to becoming acquainted with those you don't normally spend time with, feel free, of course, to meet more people of the kind you already know that you like. Both kinds of outreach are good ways of learning to love more people.

Why might such experiences make you more loving? For many people, feeling love for others requires first finding something appealing about them. Let's imagine that you have just chosen to spend time with a person whose appearance doesn't appeal to you. In the course of a conversation, this individual might tell you a story about his or her life that you find fascinating, a story that teaches an important lesson that you need to learn. At that moment, the experience may generate an initial spark of love that can gradually grow into the greater love of appreciating each person as a uniquely created child of God, one with whom God intended you to spend time and to love. Should you do this kind of outreach often enough, you might eventually learn to be curious about God's plan for someone you see for the first time and to have an immediate desire to treat her or him as an honored guest at a great event as one excellent way of becoming acquainted. Perhaps, then, someday you'll host the kind of feast described in Luke 14:12-14 (NKJV). Praise God when you do!

Live the Gospel by Loving More People

Just as your daily travels could either be limited to the interior of your home or, instead, involve going to many of the same places, choosing to love more people means extending your presence and yourself to do so. The following questions should help you to have the desire and commitment to make that effort each day:

1. How did you come to love those you love now?

2. How could you repeat those steps to find more people to love?

3. What kinds of people have you never loved?

4. How might you develop love for at least one such person?

5. What can you do today to start the process of developing love for another person you don't love now?

6. What other ways might you learn to love others?

7. How can you locate more of such ways?

8. What aspects of not loving others do you need to ask God to remove from you?

9. Where can you go now to find a new person you can learn to love and want to serve?

10. What was that experience like?

11. When will you do so again?

Week One Memory Verse

"For whoever does the will of My Father in heaven is My brother and sister and mother." (Matthew 12:50, NKJV)

Week Two: Days One and Two

Love Those You Dislike

Then He went out again by the sea; and
all the multitude came to Him, and He taught them.
As He passed by, He saw Levi the son of Alphaeus
sitting at the tax office.
And He said to him, "Follow Me."
So he arose and followed Him.

Now it happened, as He was dining in Levi's house,
that many tax collectors and sinners also sat together
with Jesus and His disciples;
for there were many, and they followed Him.

And when the scribes and Pharisees saw Him eating
with the tax collectors and sinners, they said to His disciples,
"How is it that He eats and drinks
with tax collectors and sinners?"

When Jesus heard it, He said to them,
"Those who are well have no need of a physician,
but those who are sick.
I did not come to call the righteous, but sinners, to repentance."

— Mark 2:13-17 (NKJV)

Scribes and Pharisees typically avoided contact with those who were not following God's commands and the traditions of the Jewish people. In those days, tax collectors were extremely unpopular because they often took advantage of their authority to overcharge for taxes due to Rome, keeping the excess proceeds for their own benefit, while adding to the treasury of the hated conquering empire that ruled over the Jews.

In this powerful example, Jesus invited a Roman tax collector to follow Him. Levi (also known as Matthew) followed Him, and Jesus later dined at Levi's house where He met many more tax collectors and sinners. While Jesus undoubtedly hated the sins that any of these people had done and that some of them intended to keep doing, His love for these unsaved people caused Him to reach out to them to begin developing a loving relationship. We should do the same.

Notice that Jesus didn't condition His meeting such people over dinner on their having first changed their ways. Instead, He merely sought to companionably connect with them as He would have done with the most ardent believer. While the conversation was undoubtedly different from what would have been discussed with believers, the love shown was surely the same.

Any number of reasons can be presented for disliking someone. Such reasons often include behavior that is considered to be wrong, either morally or in terms of the discomfort it causes for others. In some of such cases, foul language can cause someone to be shunned. Not bathing often enough can create a similar reaction among the most fastidious about cleanliness. Being a smoker often repels those who find the odor offensive or have related health concerns. For those who are fashion conscious, another person's clothes can be a turnoff. Some trim people who exercise and diet may prefer not to look at people who are out of shape and overweight.

In making such judgments and often avoiding certain people, there's an element of pride involved. An individual who is thinking in one of such ways or taking such actions is putting his or her personal preferences ahead of Jesus' commands to love one and all.

Love can be messy. Being loving can mean getting your hands dirty, making your clothes smelly, being somewhere you feel uncomfortable, or doing something you dislike. But Jesus wouldn't have thought twice about incurring such costs when eternal consequences were involved or for an opportunity to have been in loving fellowship with a believer. We shouldn't either.

While we fall short of having the love for others that Jesus commanded, it's also easy to take a too exalted view of ourselves. I'm sure that the tax collectors could have helped the scribes and Pharisees to appreciate how their judgments of the tax collectors were making them "holier than thou," a most deplorable kind of pride. By focusing on outward show in their personal actions, rather than humbly honoring their Creator, these fault finders were also being offensive to God, just as much as if they were sinning in some other way, including whatever the tax collectors and sinners had done.

Live the Gospel by Loving Those You Dislike

Perhaps you have never considered that God would want you to love someone you now dislike. Having realized now that He does, you will need some guidance in addition to whatever you receive in response to your prayers. Use these questions to help open your heart to doing so in an ongoing way:

1. What causes you to dislike someone?

2. Are such causes ones that Jesus wants you to forgive and agreeably bear?

3. How can you adjust your attitudes so that you will spend time with those you dislike as part of seeking ways to appreciate and love them as they are?

4. How can you become more likeable to those you have disliked?

5. How can spending time with those you would have previously disliked help you to become more humble?

6. With whom could you spend time today that you have avoided in the past due to disliking something about the person?

7. How can you make that connection happen today?

8. How can you show love to this person?

9. Do you pray daily for the Holy Spirit to transform you in this way?

10. How did this experience make you feel?

11. How can you best maintain your pursuit of loving people you once would have disliked?

Week Two Memory Verse

"I did not come to call *the* righteous, but sinners, to repentance." (Mark 2:17, NKJV)

Week Two: Days Three and Four

Love Those Who Have Hurt You

"To him who strikes you on the one cheek,
offer the other also.
And from him who takes away your cloak,
do not withhold your tunic either."

"But if you love those who love you,
what credit is that to you?
For even sinners love those who love them."

— Luke 6:29, 32 (NKJV)

Jesus' direction to tolerate abuse from others without retaliating is hard to follow. Most people want to "get even." With the passage of time, anger can sometimes abate sufficiently so that no retribution is ever sought. But how can we possibly then move beyond having such a reduced amount of anger to unreservedly loving those "who did us wrong"? The challenge is especially great because the most painful hurts often come from those who are closest to us. The sense of betrayal in such cases can leave such a searing pain that it seems impossible to erase.

Many Bible verses tell us that much is impossible for humans, and most people are all too aware of their own limitations. However, we need to remember that all impossible things are actually possible with God's help. Consequently, pray for His guidance in forgiving and loving those who have hurt you.

While no two ways of accomplishing such difficult transformations may be the same, keep in mind that changing will often be easier if you first focus on just one person who has hurt you in only one way on just one occasion. Much in the way that you might start exercising with simple, easy, and brief activities, look for opportunities to take on such a limited, focused challenge that should be less difficult for you than the greater ones. Obviously, if two people have hurt you in one way on one occasion, but to different degrees, you should first seek to forgive and love the person who caused you the lesser hurt.

As we addressed in Part One during week four, days three through six, the first step is to forgive. You will always feel easier about doing so if you recall the example of Jesus on the cross as He asked God to forgive His persecutors and mockers, "Father, forgive them, for they do not know what they do" (Luke 23:34, NKJV). Notice that Jesus asked for them to be forgiven in a way that enabled the listening offenders to know that He had forgiven them. Be sure that those you have forgiven learn of your forgiveness, as well.

Once you have forgiven the person who hurt you, it's time to connect with the person in a way that positively reflects your forgiveness of her or him. So you should not be cold or unfriendly to this person. You should, instead, be eagerly seeking to develop a loving relationship as good as you have with anyone else. Doing so will be a wonderful test of whether you have really forgiven the person. Much prayer will undoubtedly be required to prepare, strengthen, and direct you in doing so.

Having accomplished such a good result, then begin the process again with a different person who has hurt you. Realize that God will probably lead you in a different way to accomplish this next result. And keep going until you have done so with all those who have hurt you.

Live the Gospel by Loving Those Who Have Hurt You

If loving those you previously disliked seemed incomprehensible to you, perhaps you now find growing to love those who have hurt you to be even more difficult to imagine and accomplish. The following questions are designed to help you begin to develop experiences that will make this transformation possible and permanent:

1. What is the slightest hurt that you have not yet forgiven?

2. How has being hurt in this way created a potential blessing for you from God?

3. Are you praying for help in forgiving the person who caused that hurt?

4. Are you doing what God directs you to do for forgiving in this case?

5. If you have forgiven any hurts, have you let the people know that you have forgiven them?

6. Do they feel forgiven by you?

7. What first step can you take today to begin building a loving relationship with someone who has hurt you and you have forgiven, whether or not you now feel love for that person?

8. What guidance has God given you for doing so?

9. How did you feel as you took this first step?

10. How can you be sure to seek loving relationships with those who hurt you in the future?

Week Two Memory Verse

"I did not come to call *the* righteous, but sinners, to repentance." (Mark 2:17, NKJV)

Week Two: Days Five and Six

Love Your Enemies

"But love your enemies,
do good, and lend, hoping for nothing in return;
and your reward will be great, and
you will be sons of the Most High.
For He is kind to the unthankful and evil."

— Luke 6:35 (NKJV)

Jesus' command in Luke 6:35 (NKJV) requires some analysis. Who is your "enemy?" As I thought about that term in the context of the Bible, I was reminded of the confrontation between David and Goliath, a situation where each one was trying to kill the other.

Fortunately, it's unlikely that anyone is actually trying to kill you today. If someone were so engaged, it's clear, of course, that person is your *enemy*. There may also be people who seek to permanently harm you in some physical way, such as a driver enraged by something you did. However, there could be other people who would simply be pleased if they heard that you had been killed or injured, despite such individuals planning no action to accomplish such a result. Others may simply want to take advantage of you to gain some tangible benefit, such as by stealing your identity.

In ordinary parlance, an *opponent* is often thought of as someone who puts his or her personal interests ahead of ours in either word or deed. If someone does so frequently, an "opponent" can turn into an "enemy" in our minds. However, there's little chance that a person using such a mental perspective will become physically dangerous to you or anyone else. In addition, someone who opposes us from time to time can also be thought of as an enemy because of the manner in which the opposition has been conducted, particularly if it involved either aggressive or rude verbal attacks.

You may be wondering how you could possibly love any of such people. You will again have to rely on God to help you do so.

However, it may help a bit to shift your perspective by describing these individuals in another way, a more positive one. For instance, someone in an opposing army who seeks to kill you while you also serve in your own country's army can be appreciated for being faithful in following whatever is commanded by the other country's leaders. If the person is brave and effective while doing so, these are at least two more reasons for appreciating something about such an enemy.

An opponent may be faithful to a different set of beliefs from yours. We can appreciate the other person's faithfulness, in such a case, even if we don't agree with the beliefs.

Someone who is very rude to us can also be seen as someone who is upset, out of control, and lacks skills needed for politely opposing us. Seen from any of these perspectives, such an individual is someone for whom we should feel concern because of what caused the bad behavior.

In other words, there's always some reason to feel sympathy for and to approve of some aspect of an "enemy" or "opponent." But doing so is obviously not the same as loving that person. How might that transition be accomplished? God has many ways to help you do so.

One possible shift in perspective is by seeing any nonbelieving enemy as someone who needs Salvation, a person who can benefit for all eternity from our help. If the enemy or opponent is a believer, we can have similar concern that the person may not have repented any wrong behavior and thoughts with regard to us, thus blocking his or her relationship with God. A loving relationship with such a person might help repair such a broken connection to God.

Another potential shift in your perspective is to see a future saved or a repentant enemy or opponent as a future brother or sister in Christ, a potential part of our own community who will collaborate with us to expand and improve God's Kingdom. How could we not love such a person? If you doubt such a shift is possible, remember that Jesus chose Saul of Tarsus, someone who helped kill and imprison believers, to be His highly effective, untiring ambassador to the Gentiles. In doing so, we should also think of ways to speed the process of developing such a new relationship through changing our own attitudes and actions.

Beyond that, please pray for God to guide you on a path that will enable you to see each "enemy" differently and remove all barriers to feeling love for her or him.

Live the Gospel by Loving Your Enemies

Once again, this lesson calls for you to love those you may have never considered that you could love. Jesus' wonderful example can strengthen and encourage us all here. The following questions will help you find information that can guide you towards having such transformed relationships, now and in the future:

1. Who are your enemies (those who personally intend to do *you* significant harm)?

2. Who are your bitter opponents (those who take opposition to extreme levels, beyond the mere merits of the differences)?

3. Who are your temporary opponents?

4. How might you see each person you identified in answering the first three questions more favorably?

5. Have you forgiven these individuals for what they have done?

6. Do those who are forgiven know they have been forgiven by you?

7. What would a loving relationship with each one look like after the emotions stirred by the current conflicts dissipate?

8. What could you do today to begin causing those emotions to disappear and the relationships to move in the right direction?

9. How do you need to pray differently to gain the strength and direction you need to come to love all these people?

10. How did it feel to take these first steps?

11. What will you do tomorrow to build on these first steps?

Week Two Memory Verse

"I did not come to call *the* righteous, but sinners, to repentance." (Mark 2:17, NKJV)

Week Three: Days One and Two

Love God with All Your Heart

Then one of the scribes came,
and having heard them reasoning together,
perceiving that He had answered them well, asked Him,
"Which is the first commandment of all?"

Jesus answered him,
"The first of all the commandments is:
'Hear, O Israel, the LORD our God, the LORD is one.
And you shall love the LORD your God with all your heart, ….'
This is the first commandment.

"And the second, like it, is this:
'You shall love your neighbor as yourself.'
There is no other commandment greater than these."

— Mark 12:28-31 (NKJV)

A man's heart plans his way,
But the LORD directs his steps.

— Proverbs 16:9 (NKJV)

"For God so loved the world that
He gave His only begotten Son,
that whoever believes in Him should not perish
but have everlasting life."

— John 3:16 (NKJV)

Every good gift and every perfect gift is from above, and
comes down from the Father of lights,
with whom there is no variation or shadow of turning.

— James 1:17 (NKJV)

In Part Two, we have been looking at the loving relationships God wants us to have with other people. If you have had any trouble applying the prior lessons in this part, realize that at least some of the difficulty may be due to lacking sufficient love for God. To investigate this possibility, we begin by looking in this lesson at what it means to love God will all your heart.

In the Bible, the heart is considered, in part, as the seat of emotions, as well as the center for making choices (potentially even overwhelming the logic of the mind through strength of desire). Perhaps that's why the verses in Deuteronomy 6:4-5 (NKJV), part of which contains this week's memory verse, and Mark 12:28-31 (NKJV) mention loving God with all your heart first, before going on to refer to your soul, mind, and strength.

Many people characterize the Bible as describing God's search for a relationship with each of us. If left to follow their own inclinations, many people would worship themselves or chase after some aspect related to base desires that God sees as sin. By sending Jesus to die on the cross so that we can each come alive spiritually for all eternity, our Almighty Father showed love beyond anything that we could possibly do in return. When we think about the sacrifice of the Father and of the Son, we cannot help but feel our hearts wanting to embrace Them with everything that is within us.

Such love can also fill our hearts by remembering that everything good we like about the world, as well as our very lives, is a gift from God. So we should see Him whenever we contemplate, desire, or enjoy any of these good gifts, giving God full credit for His love, goodness, and generosity in providing them to us.

Live the Gospel by Loving God with All Your Heart

Most people hold back from making full emotional commitments, often out of fear of being hurt. With God, we need have no such concern. These questions are designed to help you remove barriers to giving God all of your love, now and forevermore:

1. How does having received the gift of Salvation affect your ability to fill your heart with love for God?

2. How do the good things that God has provided for you cause you to feel more love for Him in your heart?

3. If you ever feel your heart to be only partially filled with love for God, how might you expand your love for Him?

4. Do you pray daily for God to fill your heart with love for Him?

5. If you do not so pray, can you begin doing so now?

6. How does it feel to fill your heart with love for Him?

7. How do you see other people differently now?

8. Can you see other people now with the love God has for them?

Week Three Memory Verse

"Hear, O Israel: The LORD our God, the LORD *is* one!" (Deuteronomy 6:4, NKJV)

N.B.: Notice that "Hear" in this verse is in the imperative form, which implies "Hear and obey." Some Christians who understand Biblical Hebrew note that the word representing "one" (*echad*) in this verse can be used to describe a plural entity, much in the way we would say that many football players wearing the same uniform comprise a team. Consequently, in this view "one" in this quote refers to the Trinity of our Heavenly Father, His Son Jesus, and the Holy Spirit. Others with knowledge of Biblical Hebrew argue that "one" is singular and refers solely to our Heavenly Father. *Echad* is used for describing a plural entity, as well as individual ones, throughout the Old Testament. In addition, *echad* also just means "one," the first number above zero, and in this regard can simply express having the highest rank. From this perspective, this quote would suggest that God is first among all. Since Jesus is being quoted as saying so in Mark 12:28-31 (NKJV), it is reasonably likely that He was referring to our Heavenly Father and Him being first in rank. I encourage you to pray for guidance from the Holy Spirit about how to interpret Jesus' meaning here.

Week Three: Days Three and Four

Love God with All Your Soul

Then one of the scribes came,
and having heard them reasoning together,
perceiving that He had answered them well, asked Him,
"Which is the first commandment of all?"

Jesus answered him,
"The first of all the commandments is:
'Hear, O Israel, the LORD our God, the LORD is one.
And you shall love the LORD your God
with all your heart, with all your soul, ...'
This is the first commandment.

"And the second, like it, is this:
'You shall love your neighbor as yourself.'
There is no other commandment greater than these."

— Mark 12:28-31 (NKJV)

The most important point to appreciate about loving God with all of your soul is that doing so isn't separate from loving Him with all your heart, mind, and strength. Thus, you can think of what Jesus had to say in the whole of Mark 12:30 (NKJV) as telling you something like "hold back nothing from your full commitment to God and His purposes."

Let me also add a few observations about "love" as expressed in these verses. In English, this feeling can be manifested in different forms and degrees, from the love of child for a new toy to the lifelong commitment of spouses to be faithful to one another through their promises to God and one another. Jesus is talking about the kind of love that involves being willing to do what actually is, or at least seems, sacrificial at the time (even if some personal benefits are expected to eventually be received) because of a strong desire to do the best for the loved one.

Some people equate "soul" with "spirit," but some Bible scholars would disagree. Instead, think of "soul" in this context as meaning the intangible qualities that bring life to a human body. Perceiving this meaning may perhaps be best understood by considering that when the soul is gone, the person's body no longer holds physical life.

If we take this view of what a soul is, how should this command about the soul be interpreted? In one sense, the command means committing all of the body's actions to serving God in doing His will. As you can see, this aspect of a commitment to God is much different from simply having strong feelings in favor of serving Him, as would occur with only having a heart-based commitment. With regard to this soul-based dimension of Mark 12:30 (NKJV), we are talking about putting a whole life into a Godly harness to take action.

At a deeper level, the same concept of soul can also tell us that we should think about how we can best serve God whenever we choose to direct our lives in any way.

When we consider these two perspectives (all actions for His purposes and choosing to best serve God) together, it becomes more obvious why this verse's command puts the heart and soul ahead of mentioning the mind and strength of a person. With the commitment of the heart and the actions of the entire body as represented by the soul, the person's mind and strength will undoubtedly follow at least to some extent. The opposite order would not be equally likely to create as fruitful results.

Live the Gospel by Loving God with All Your Soul

It's obviously a big step to go from dedicating part of your life to God (such as when you only attend services on Sunday) to then applying *all* of your life to Him. Perhaps you will find it easier to start doing so by making such commitments for shorter durations than all the time. As you experience the delight of doing more for God, your reactions to the experiences should help you transition to loving Him with your whole soul. These questions should help you make such a transition from where you are now in loving God to increasing towards a full commitment of time and actions to Him in a loving relationship:

1. How does having received the gift of Salvation affect your ability to love God with all your soul?

2. How do the good things that God has provided for you cause you to love Him in a way that commits more parts of your life to Him?

3. If you have ever felt your soul to be solely directed by love of God, what might you think or do to extend this commitment into directing more aspects of your life?

4. Are there any parts of your life that you haven't yet surrendered in love to Him?

5. Do you pray daily for God to help you direct your life so that your soul will be fully committed to acting as He wishes because of your love for Him?

6. If you do not so pray, can you begin now to do so?

7. How did increasing your commitment to and actions for God today change your love for Him and others?

8. How can you best maintain as much love for God as possible in your soul?

Week Three Memory Verse

"Hear, O Israel: The LORD our God, the LORD *is* one!" (Deuteronomy 6:4, NKJV)

Week Three: Days Five and Six

Love God with All Your Mind

Then one of the scribes came,
and having heard them reasoning together,
perceiving that He had answered them well, asked Him,
"Which is the first commandment of all?"

Jesus answered him,
"The first of all the commandments is:
'Hear, O Israel, the LORD our God, the LORD is one.
And you shall love the LORD your God
with all your heart, with all your soul,
with all your mind, ….'
This is the first commandment.

"And the second, like it, is this:
'You shall love your neighbor as yourself.'
There is no other commandment greater than these."

— Mark 12:28-31 (NKJV)

In addressing the concept of "mind" here, we need to remember that knowledge of twenty-first century neurology and psychology were not then understood by Jesus' hearers. Instead, these listeners would have probably equated "mind" to the thinking of a person. Because of having total sacrificial love for God, such a hearer might imagine that the influence of this love would adjust a believer's thoughts and ideas to reflect His perspective, as expressed by today's Bible. Once again, let me remind you that the four included elements in Mark 12:30 (NKJV) — heart, soul, mind, and strength — are cumulative rather than individual. That's the apparent purpose of having them listed as they are in the verse.

Let me give you an example of what such total commitment could look like. Let's imagine that you regularly do the grocery shopping for your family. Normally, your thoughts about this activity might focus on checking the cupboard and refrigerator to see what items need to be replenished, looking for coupons to cut costs, and planning a time to go that would shorten the task's duration. I'm sure you've done such or similar thinking and actions on many occasions.

If your thinking were, instead, totally devoted to loving and serving God, you would first focus on how you might expand and improve God's Kingdom by your grocery shopping. With such a focus, you might consider what you could buy to share with a neighbor you are witnessing to, how you might acquire and then contribute some food and household supplies to the needy, and how you might create opportunities to share your testimony with those who will be present while you shop.

Do you see the differences? In the first instance, you were only thinking about what to do in terms of your own self-interest and efficiency. In the second case, you were letting all of your self-interest take a back seat to serving God's Kingdom as you planned what to do.

If you apply this kind of thinking to whatever you do, I'm sure you'll soon see that your priorities will undergo a big change, and you will be engaging in many new activities while you perform your usual ones. For instance, at work you will probably do more to set a good example and be kind to one and all, rather than trying so hard to impress the boss to earn a promotion and receive a higher income.

If you did receive a larger income, for example, you would probably then think about how you could use the added funds to advance God's purposes, rather than planning to use all the increase to benefit yourself and your family, such as by buying a nicer house to live in and fancier vehicle to drive yourself. Be sure to apply such a changed perspective to all aspects of your thinking and deciding.

Live the Gospel by Loving God with All Your Mind

Romans 12:1-2 (NKJV) has good directions for what is required: "I beseech you therefore, brethren, by the mercies of God, that you present your bodies a living sacrifice, holy, acceptable to God, *which is* your reasonable service. And do not be conformed to this world, but be transformed by the renewing of your mind, that you may prove what *is* that good and acceptable and perfect will of God." Here are some questions designed to help you engage in such a total mental renewal based on having sacrificial love for God:

1. Have you kept a record lately of how you spend all of your daily time? If you haven't, please do so beginning today.

2. After you have been keeping track of your ways of spending time for at least a week, look at your record and ask, "In which of these activities did my thinking cause me to put God's purposes first in how I engaged in what I did?"

3. For any activities where you did not put God's purposes first ask, "How do I need to change how I plan and perform my activities to *always* put God's purposes first?"

4. Where you are unsure of what God's purposes are for such an activity, ask God, "What do you want me to do while I engage in such an activity?"

5. Daily review your record of how well you have put God's purposes first in your thinking and planning for each activity. Ask God then, "How did I do today?" and "What must I do differently tomorrow to overcome any places where I put my needs ahead of Your purposes?"

6. How do you experience life differently now that you are putting God first in your thinking?

7. How can you continue to shift your thinking in these ways?

Week Three Memory Verse

"Hear, O Israel: The LORD our God, the LORD *is* one!" (Deuteronomy 6:4, NKJV)

Week Four: Days One and Two

Love God with All Your Strength

Then one of the scribes came,
and having heard them reasoning together,
perceiving that He had answered them well, asked Him,
"Which is the first commandment of all?"

Jesus answered him,
"The first of all the commandments is:
'Hear, O Israel, the LORD our God, the LORD is one.
And you shall love the LORD your God
with all your heart, with all your soul,
with all your mind, and with all your strength.'
This is the first commandment.

"And the second, like it, is this:
'You shall love your neighbor as yourself.'
There is no other commandment greater than these."

— Mark 12:28-31 (NKJV)

Of the four elements in Mark 12:30 (NKJV) we have been discussing, the concept of "strength" is probably the easiest one for us to appreciate in a way similar to how the original hearers did: You are to simply apply all your energy to whatever the combination of your heart, soul, and mind direct you to do for God because you love Him. Perhaps an illustration will help. We've all seen a young child reluctantly respond to a command or request to pick up and clean her or his room. Such a child drags around slowly, doesn't do a very good job, and acts grumpy while and after doing so. By contrast, someone who loves cleanliness and order will do the same task with a bright smile, considerable energy, and a quick step. The results will look quite a bit better, as well.

Someone who has made such a willing commitment to God and His purposes is also likely to have worked on increasing his or her strength so that more can be accomplished. Having more strength will also potentially expand the ability of the heart, soul, and mind to be constant in applying the available strength, due to being relieved of any concerns about being physically overwhelmed or endangered while performing a task.

It can also be quite encouraging to feel fully engaged in doing something worthwhile. Having applied all of one's strength to a task is also helpful for concentrating attention and creating a happy sense of fulfillment related to having done one's best.

While the verse addresses just the elements of heart, soul, mind, and strength, if there are other aspects of you that can be committed to expressing your unlimited love for God, feel free to add those elements, as well.

Live the Gospel by Loving God with All Your Strength

In considering how to love God with all your strength, separately evaluate the strength dimensions of intensity, duration, and consistency as you answer each of the following questions:

1. When have you been able to love God with your entire strength by utilizing it for serving Him or His Kingdom?

2. What lessons have such experiences provided for loving with and applying more strength?

3. How has God already expanded your strength for doing specific tasks?

4. What are the lessons from these experiences for further expanding your strength?

5. What hinders you from concentrating your strength on loving God in some instances?

6. How could such hindrances be overcome?

7. What can you do now to expand, concentrate, and apply more of your strength to God's purposes with all your love?

8. How did you feel after doing one or more of those things?

9. How can you sustain adding to and applying more strength to God's purposes with the power of all your love?

Week Four Memory Verse

"'… [I]nasmuch as you did *it* to one of the least of these My brethren, you did *it* to Me.'" (Matthew 25:40, NKJV)

Week Four: Days Three and Four

Do Good to Those You Encounter

But he, wanting to justify himself, said to Jesus,
"And who is my neighbor?"

Then Jesus answered and said:
"A certain man *went down from Jerusalem to Jericho, and*
fell among thieves, who stripped him of his clothing,
wounded him, *and departed, leaving* him *half dead.*

"Now by chance a certain priest came down that road.
And when he saw him, he passed by on the other side.

"Likewise a Levite, when he arrived at the place,
came and looked, and passed by on the other side.

"But a certain Samaritan, as he journeyed, came where he was.
And when he saw him, he had compassion.
So he went to him *and bandaged his wounds, pouring on oil and wine;*
and he set him on his own animal, brought him to an inn,
and took care of him. On the next day, when he departed,
he took out two denarii, gave them *to the innkeeper, and said to him,*
'Take care of him; and whatever more you spend,
when I come again, I will repay you.'

"So which of these three do you think was neighbor
to him who fell among the thieves?"

And he said, "He who showed mercy on him."

Then Jesus said to him, "Go and do likewise."

— Luke 10:29-37 (NKJV)

In the Parable of the Good Samaritan (Luke 10:30-37, NKJV), we see that Jesus directed the questioner to view anyone he came into contact with as a "neighbor," one to whom love is owed, as stated in Mark 12:31 (NKJV): "And the second, like *it, is* this: 'You shall love your neighbor as yourself.' There is no other commandment greater than these."

Most people certainly act as if they love themselves quite a bit, lavishing much more of their time, effort, and money on personal comfort, preferences, and interests than in meeting the needs of others. Should such a degree of self-love be applied, as well, to neighbors (those we come into contact with at any time), surely such beneficiaries would find themselves well treated.

Who are those we encounter? Well, it's clear from the parable that anyone in need who is close enough that we can help them is such a neighbor. For instance, if you were eating in a restaurant, looked out the window, and noticed someone fall on the sidewalk outside, you should get up, go out, and see how you can help the fallen person. Perhaps no assistance might be needed, but you would certainly want someone to check on you if you had just fallen, wouldn't you? If help is required, your action might be very much appreciated, even if you have no practical skills for assisting and simply speak kind words in a soothing tone to the person while waiting for expert assistance to arrive.

As the parable suggests, the person who needs help might not be in a position to ask for aid due to having been injured, not being able to speak at the moment, or feeling shy about reaching out. Think of yourself as the "love" provider for those who need some of it but do not ask (which is pretty much everyone who isn't both in a close relationship with Jesus and having a great day in every way).

This lesson emphasizes doing something helpful for the neighbor in need, as does the Parable of the Good Samaritan. As you probably appreciate, in telling this parable Jesus seemed to have been encouraging love of neighbors. Why did He provide such encouragement in this way? While we certainly don't know for sure, one possibility is that Jesus realized that it's hard for us to love a stranger. However, as soon as we spend time with someone, at least some love for a person will usually develop. In caring for someone who obviously needs help, compassion could surely develop while doing what we can to assist. That compassion, in turn, can grow into viewing the person in need with sacrificial love. If we help in such ways often enough, perhaps we can eventually see all strangers as being among those Jesus wants us to love, whether or not they appear to have any immediate needs we can meet.

Live the Gospel by Doing Good to All You Encounter

As you begin to act in this way, realize that you will be spending more time doing many tasks, simply because you will be adding new activities to help others while engaged in whatever you usually do. Be sure to adjust your expectations about what you can accomplish while you are with others. If you don't, the joy that Jesus intends for you to feel from assisting others will be offset by anxiety as you fall behind your plans for accomplishing other tasks. Here are questions designed to help you begin to notice and more often act on what you notice to do good for others:

1. When have you applied the Parable of the Good Samaritan to sacrificially help a stranger?

2. How did such experiences affect your love for anyone you helped?

3. What has kept you from sacrificially helping strangers more often?

4. What would have to change about your thinking and behavior to notice more "neighbors" who aren't yet known to you and to find ways to help them that would ultimately cause you to feel more loving towards them?

5. Who can you do something loving for today for the very first time among those you encounter?

6. Did you do so?

7. What was your feeling from having helped someone for the very first time?

8. Who else can you take such actions with?

9. How can you ensure that you will continue to do so?

Week Four Memory Verse

"'... [I]nasmuch as you did *it* to one of the least of these My brethren, you did *it* to Me.'" (Matthew 25:40, NKJV)

Week Four: Days Five and Six

Do Good to Those You Will Never Meet

*"'… [I]nasmuch as you did it to one of the least of these My brethren,
you did it to Me.'"*

— Matthew 25:40 (NKJV)

*And when He was already not far from the house,
the centurion sent friends to Him, saying to Him,*

*"Lord, do not trouble Yourself, for I am not worthy
that You should enter under my roof.
Therefore I did not even think myself worthy
to come to You. But say the word,
and my servant will be healed."*

— Luke 7:6-7 (NKJV)

Distance healing is rarely mentioned in the Bible. Instead, in-person interventions are usually described. However, in Luke 7:6-7 (NKJV) we see a Gentile, a Roman centurion, who expressed faith that Jesus need only command that his servant would be healed and that would occur, whether or not Jesus ever came into contact with the servant. Jesus directed the healing from afar, and He marveled that He had not found such great faith as the centurion had among those in Israel.

Today, we don't need supernatural powers to help some of those we will never meet. Humanitarian organizations of all kinds serve the most desperate and poorest people around the world. Unless you never pay any attention to the mail you receive, what's on the Internet, or the news, you will eventually be given many opportunities to supply money as a way to meet some of the needs of those served by such organizations.

Matthew 25:40 (NKJV) indicates that whatever is done to help is as if it had been done directly to Jesus. Naturally, I'm sure you would love to have an opportunity to do something beneficial for your Lord and Savior that He would appreciate.

Realizing how many potential opportunities there are to serve people in need whom you will never meet can make you feel a bit overwhelmed. Obviously, you cannot do more in providing for others than your resources permit. Ask God to tell you how much you should provide in this way.

While money is one obvious way to accomplish helpful results, notice that prayer can also be a way to help provide for those in need, especially for those who also don't know Jesus as their Lord and Savior. Such prayers can be directed for provision, along with a request that the results help draw those who benefit closer to Jesus.

Between those extremes of tangible and intangible ways to help is the additional option of volunteering time and efforts to directly or indirectly serve those in need. For instance, some humanitarian organizations near you might need people to do volunteer tasks that serve the needy (such as feeding the homeless in a shelter) or attract more supporters (perhaps by providing information one Sunday at your church).

Clearly, you should pray about who and how God wants you to serve among those who are the "least" of our current and potential brothers and sisters in Christ. For some people, doing so could turn out to be an important aspect of their calling from God. When that combination of calling and service occurs, life with Jesus will clearly become much more abundant for the person so engaged.

Live the Gospel by Doing Good to Those You Will Never Meet

Rather than feeling overwhelmed by the magnitude and variety of the opportunities to help those you will never meet, the following questions are designed to lead you towards what God intends for you to always be doing in this regard:

1. When have you provided directly or indirectly for the needs of those you will never meet?

2. How did such experiences affect your love for the people you helped?

3. What has kept you from sacrificially helping more often in more ways?

4. What would have to change about your thinking and behavior to notice more people you will never meet and ways to help them that would cause you to feel more loving towards them?

5. Who can you do something loving for today, for the very first time, to help someone you will never meet?

6. For whom else can you take this and other actions to help today?

7. How did you feel before, during, and after you helped?

8. How can you ensure that you will do so whenever God calls you in this way?

Week Four Memory Verse

"'... [I]nasmuch as you did *it* to one of the least of these My brethren, you did *it* to Me.'" (Matthew 25:40, NKJV)

Week Five: Days One and Two

Do Good to Those You Used to Dislike

As Peter was coming in, Cornelius met him and
fell down at his feet and worshiped him.

But Peter lifted him up, saying,
"Stand up; I myself am also a man."

And as he talked with him, he went in
and found many who had come together.

Then he said to them,
"You know how unlawful it is for a Jewish man
to keep company with or go to one of another nation.
But God has shown me that I should not call
any man common or unclean.
Therefore I came without objection
as soon as I was sent for.
I ask, then, for what reason have you sent for me?"

— Acts 10:25-29 (NKJV)

Dislike can be based in many circumstances. In Acts 10:25-29 (NKJV), we see that the Apostle Peter had overcome his desire to avoid those who were not Jewish because of the custom prohibiting such contact. God helped in this regard by showing Peter that such distinctions should not be made. In this chapter of Acts, Peter is now ready and willing to help someone he would once have avoided.

As we explored in week two, days one and two of this part, many reasons for dislike have an even less sound foundation than the prescriptions of Jewish traditions and law originally had for Peter. For instance, someone who merely appeared to be different from you might make you feel as if you had a reason to dislike that person. As an example, you might have been brought up to believe that wearing certain kinds of clothes (such as those that are too revealing) reflects poor morals. Or, you might believe that you could never do other than dislike someone who disagrees with one of your strong personal beliefs. Someone who even speaks more loudly than you prefer could also stimulate a sense of disliking in you.

Three kinds of experiences can help you overcome such dislikes: Appreciating that God wants us to love those we dislike, getting to know the person's good characteristics, and developing a relationship with the person through serving him or her. Let's begin by appreciating that God wants us to love everyone. If you search the New Testament, you won't find a place where Jesus said that it was all right to do anything other than love everyone, regardless of whether there is or might be anything offensive about that person.

So, having worked on overcoming our dislikes, we need to focus now on doing good things for those who were once on our "bad" lists. As you do, keep in mind that simply forgetting the reason you once disliked someone is a great way to become more willing to do good things for her or him.

Remember that we are directed by Jesus to go beyond merely doing what's expected, even for those who mistreat us. As an example, consider Luke 6:29-30 (NKJV): "To him who strikes you on the *one* cheek, offer the other also. And from him who takes away your cloak, do not withhold *your* tunic either. Give to everyone who asks of you. And from him who takes away your goods do not ask *them* back." After reading these verses, it doesn't take much imagination to realize that Jesus called for doing good to someone you once disliked.

Keep in mind that doing good can then help you begin establishing a loving relationship. In many instances, those you once disliked were aware of your prior attitude. As a result, it will take more than just stopping any hostile actions and disgusted facial expressions to reach the point where you would normally be with someone you had just met. So your good actions will benefit the person you formerly disliked, as well as you, by establishing the right kind of relationship now that your attitude has been transformed.

Live the Gospel by Doing Good to Those You Used to Dislike

To overcome any reluctance you have to help those you used to dislike, the following questions are intended to give you a fresh start in thinking about and doing good for them:

1. When have you directly or indirectly provided or done something good for someone you previously disliked?

2. How did such experiences affect your love for and relationships with the people you helped?

3. What has kept you from more often sacrificially helping those and other such people?

4. What would have to change about your thinking and behavior to feel more loving towards more people you used to dislike while actively providing benefits for them?

5. For whom among those you used to dislike can you do something loving for today for the very first time?

6. For whom else among those you used to dislike can you take this and other beneficial actions today?

7. What did the experience feel like?

8. How can you ensure that you will do so whenever God wants you to?

Week Five Memory Verse

"If your enemy is hungry, give him bread to eat;
And if he is thirsty, give him water to drink; …." (Proverbs 25:21, NKJV)

Week Five: Days Three and Four

Do Good to Those Who Have Hurt You

"Blessed are *the merciful,*
For they shall obtain mercy."

"Blessed are *those who are*
persecuted for righteousness' sake,
For theirs is the kingdom of heaven.
Blessed are you when they revile and persecute you, and
say all kinds of evil against you falsely for My sake.
Rejoice and be exceedingly glad,
for great is *your reward in heaven,*
for so they persecuted the prophets
who were before you."

— Matthew 5:7, 10-12 (NKJV)

As we recognized during days three and four of week two in this part, Luke 23:34 (NKJV) indicates how Jesus prayed for forgiveness for those who had just crucified Him, as well as those who were there scoffing and being entertained by His suffering: "Then Jesus said, 'Father, forgive them, for they do not know what they do.'" Obviously, He was showing mercy. And earlier, in the Beatitudes, Jesus related that either having been attacked or persecuted for the sake of righteousness or because of upholding Jesus is a blessing that will provide rewards in heaven. He praised the merciful in the same message. Clearly, we are to look past our hurts and be merciful, as He has been and is merciful.

Once someone who has hurt you physically or emotionally realizes that he or she needs mercy from you, there may be no better deed you can do for that person than to be merciful … even if all you do is to completely forgive and forget the wrong. Beyond that, you can clearly indicate that you love this person who once hurt you by kindly doing something to benefit her or him. Doing so, in turn, can either help lead a nonbeliever to gain Salvation or a believer to do good works with love for others.

Remembering that many of those who have hurt us the most are either family members or friends, changing the relationship by freely giving good gifts of time, attention, encouragement, and practical aid can help establish a new foundation for being on friendly terms, a foundation that you should seek to make similar in lovingness and fruitfulness to the one that you have with Jesus.

Live the Gospel by Doing Good to Those Who Have Hurt You

Rather than feel conflicted about helping those who have hurt you, please use the following questions to see and address this opportunity in fresh and encouraging ways:

1. When have you directly or indirectly provided benefits for someone who had previously hurt you?

2. How did such experiences affect your love for and relationships with the people you helped?

3. What has kept you from sacrificially helping such people more often?

4. What would have to change about your thinking and behavior for you to lovingly help more of the people who have hurt you?

5. For whom among those who once hurt you can you do something loving today for the very first time?

6. For whom else among those who once hurt you can you today take this and other beneficial actions?

7. How did doing so feel?

8. How can you ensure that you will do so whenever God wants you to?

Week Five Memory Verse

"If your enemy is hungry, give him bread to eat;
And if he is thirsty, give him water to drink; ...." (Proverbs 25:21, NKJV)

Week Five: Days Five and Six

Do Good to Your Enemies

If your enemy is hungry, give him bread to eat;
And if he is thirsty, give him water to drink; ....

— Proverbs 25:21 (NKJV)

Week five's memory verse perfectly introduces this lesson's subject. Proverbs 25:21 (NKJV) directs us to provide for the needs of our enemies. As you think about this topic, keep in mind what you learned about loving your enemies during the lesson on days five and six of week two in this part.

Clearly, we are not to love our enemies from afar, but up close and personal, to meet their needs, perhaps even in our own homes. While no one knows for sure why doing so is directed, it's always helpful to speculate a bit about how God's Kingdom is enhanced by our doing something He directs. One possibility is that providing for an enemy's needs can create the potential for a more lasting peace. In addition, there is also the possibility that an enemy who isn't a believer in Jesus might become interested in developing such faith. Further, imagine that fierce enemies could become allies who seek to do good together. Clearly, should that happy result occur neither of the new allies will need to put as much effort into self-protection. Moreover, much good can be accomplished for those who most need the help. If thinking about all these potentialities seems abstract, imagine that David and Goliath had teamed up and the Israelites and the Philistines had also become allies. Certainly, the history of Israel from that time forward would undoubtedly have been quite different … perhaps even leading to the Israelites seeking to attract nations outside the Promised Land into following God.

In modern businesses, some experts argue for strong competitors finding ways to cooperate that build on their individual strengths to minimize their individual weaknesses. Where such collaboration is legal, doing so can certainly be productive.

Being on anything other than completely good terms with someone else is certainly opposed to what Jesus wants us to do. He will forgive anyone who repents of any wrong that has been thought or done. We should follow His good example on the cross, where He asked God to forgive those who had just crucified Him, as well as those who came to watch His agony as a perverse form of "entertainment" and to mock Him … thus, providing for a critical need that many of those present didn't even realize they had.

Live the Gospel by Doing Good to Those Who Are Your Enemies

Rather than wonder about what to do that would benefit your enemies, the following questions are designed to help you reach out to God and find out what He wants you to do now and in the future for serving their needs:

1. When have you directly or indirectly provided helpful benefits in a kind way to an enemy?

2. How did such experiences affect your love for and relationships with the people you helped?

3. What has kept you from sacrificially helping such people more often?

4. What would have to change about your thinking and behavior for you to lovingly help more people who are your enemies?

5. For which of your enemies can you do something loving today to provide for their needs for the very first time?

6. With whom else among your enemies can you take this and other beneficial actions today?

7. What did it feel like before, during, and after these experiences?

8. How can you ensure that you will do so whenever God wants you to provide for the needs of your enemies?

Week Five Memory Verse

"If your enemy is hungry, give him bread to eat;
And if he is thirsty, give him water to drink; ...." (Proverbs 25:21, NKJV)

Part Three:

Draw Closer to
Our Heavenly Father,
the Lord Jesus Christ, and
the Holy Spirit

"If you then, being evil, know how to give good gifts to your children,
how much more will your *heavenly Father give*
the Holy Spirit to those who ask Him!"

— Luke 11:13 (NKJV)

Blessed be *the God and Father of our Lord Jesus Christ,*
who according to His abundant mercy has begotten us again
to a living hope through the resurrection of Jesus Christ
from the dead, to an inheritance incorruptible and undefiled
and that does not fade away, reserved in heaven for you,
who are kept by the power of God through faith
for salvation ready to be revealed in the last time.
In this you greatly rejoice, though now for a little while,
if need be, you have been grieved by various trials,
that the genuineness of your faith,
being *much more precious than gold that perishes,*
though it is tested by fire, may be found to
praise, honor, and glory at the revelation of Jesus Christ,
whom having not seen you love.
Though now you do not see Him,
yet believing, you rejoice with
joy inexpressible and full of glory,
receiving the end of your faith — salvation of your *souls.*

— 1 Peter 1:3-9 (NKJV)

The verses above touch on many reasons why we should want to draw closer to our Heavenly Father, His Son, and the Holy Spirit. Our Heavenly Father wants to give us good gifts, and He has already sent His Son as one of those good gifts to make our Salvation possible. The faithfulness of Jesus in dying on the cross has provided our way to be in a personal relationship with our Heavenly Father, the Holy Spirit, and Him. Our Heavenly Father has also given us the great gift of the Holy Spirit who dwells within us after we accept the free gift of Salvation and from there provides us with much knowledge, direction, and power.

Yet many people don't know how to become closer to our Heavenly Father, Jesus, and the Holy Spirit. If you have questions in that regard, this part of *Disciple* will provide many answers, direct you to experiences that will help you draw closer, and then assist in establishing an intimacy that will enable still greater closeness to follow.

You might wonder why this topic is the third part of *Disciple*, rather than being placed earlier in the book. If that question interests you, consider by how much your awareness of God has increased through applying the lessons of the first two parts, as well as how much more closely you are following the commands of Jesus than you were just a few weeks ago. Through making these changes, you have cleared away many obstacles to your drawing closer to our Heavenly Father, His Son, and the Holy Spirit.

Let's look first at the qualities of our Heavenly Father, the Lord Jesus Christ, and the Holy Spirit that affect your potential relationships with each of Them. In doing so, I am sure you will gain still more reasons and a stronger desire to draw closer to Them.

Week One: Days One and Two

Learn the Qualities of Our Heavenly Father

So Jesus said to him, "Why do you call Me good?
No one is good but One, that is, God."

— Luke 18:19 (NKJV)

"God is Spirit, and those who worship Him
must worship in spirit and truth."

— John 4:24 (NKJV)

"The LORD your God in your midst,
The Mighty One, will save;
He will rejoice over you with gladness,
He will quiet you with His love,
He will rejoice over you with singing."

— Zephaniah 3:17 (NKJV)

Blessed be the God and Father of our Lord Jesus Christ,
who has blessed us with every spiritual blessing
in the heavenly places in Christ, just as He chose us
in Him before the foundation of the world,
that we should be holy and
without blame before Him in love,
having predestined us to adoption
as sons by Jesus Christ to Himself,
according to the good pleasure of His will,
to the praise of the glory of His grace,
by which He made us accepted in the Beloved.

— Ephesians 1:3-6 (NKJV)

*Every good gift and every perfect gift is from above, and
comes down from the Father of lights,
with whom there is no variation or shadow of turning.*

— James 1:17 (NKJV)

As physical and spiritual beings, understanding the implications of God being a spiritual being can require some mind-bending contortions. If you consider, instead, that a spiritual being has none of the physical restrictions that affect our human bodies, you can begin to appreciate that our omnipresent Heavenly Father must be a spiritual being. That is why He can always be close to us. In a few cases in the Bible, however, He chose to appear in physical form to someone, indicating that He can change in that way.

By creating us in His image, we gained our spiritual dimensions, in which our Heavenly Father has granted us every possible blessing, including a way for us to be holy through His Son Jesus. When that state is achieved through gaining Salvation and continuing repentance, we become the beloved adopted sons and daughters of our Heavenly Father.

Our Heavenly Father has none of the weaknesses, flaws, or blind spots of any human parent. Instead, He is the model of what all parents should be.

Why did He do all this? Well, He is totally good and permanently so. He has plans to do perfect things for us because of His infinite love, fulfilling His plans that pre-exist our births. Those plans include Him, as well as His Son Jesus and the Holy Spirit, being in a relationship with us.

So as saved people, we can walk in His love and with His unlimited support on paths that lead to greater fruitfulness, joy, and peace.

Why wouldn't you want to draw closer now in love to your Heavenly Father?

Draw Closer to Our Heavenly Father, the Lord Jesus Christ, and the Holy Spirit by Learning the Qualities of Our Heavenly Father

Each of us has had different experiences with our Heavenly Father. How we reacted to those experiences has varied, as well. As a result, each of us has a different degree of closeness to Him. Regardless of where this relationship is now, He wants to be closer to you. The following questions are designed to help you draw closer through experiences that wonderfully demonstrate His qualities:

1. As you read this lesson's verses, what aspects of our Heavenly Father's qualities were new to you?

2. How does considering those qualities affect your desire to experience and know Him more fully?

3. As you read those verses, were there any aspects of God that struck you as being more important?

4. If yes, how does sensing greater importance for those qualities influence how you think about and feel towards our Heavenly Father?

5. How can you more completely worship Him in spirit and in truth?

6. What would you like to say to Him now, for the first time?

7. How did what you said just now change how close you feel to Him?

8. What can you do differently today to increase your awareness of His presence?

9. How did those changes affect your closeness to Him?

10. How will you focus on drawing closer to Him in the future?

Week One Memory Verse

"Every good gift and every perfect gift is from above, and comes down from the Father of lights, …." (James 1:17, NKJV)

Week One: Days Three and Four

Learn the Qualities of the Lord Jesus Christ

And the angel answered and said to her,
"The Holy Spirit will come upon you, and
the power of the Highest will overshadow you;
therefore, also, that Holy One
who is to be born will be called the Son of God."

— Luke 1:35 (NKJV)

Jesus said to him,
"… He who has seen Me has seen the Father; …."

— John 14:9 (NKJV)

For in Him [Jesus] dwells
all the fullness of the Godhead bodily;
and you are complete in Him,
who is the head of all principality and power.

— Colossians 2:9-10 (NKJV)

He [Jesus] is the image of the invisible God,
the firstborn over all creation.
For by Him all things were created that
are in heaven and that are on earth,
visible and invisible,
whether thrones or dominions or principalities or powers.
All things were created through Him and for Him.
And He is before all things,
and in Him all things consist.
And He is the head of the body, the church,
who is the beginning, the firstborn from the dead,
that in all things He may have the preeminence.

— Colossians 1:15-18 (NKJV)

And Jesus came and spoke to them, saying,
"All authority has been given to Me
in heaven and on earth."

— Matthew 28:18 (NKJV)

… the knowledge of the mystery of God,
both of the Father and of Christ,
in whom are hidden
all the treasures of wisdom and knowledge.

— Colossians 2:2-3 (NKJV)

"For where two or three are gathered together in My name,
I am there in the midst of them."

— Matthew 18:20 (NKJV)

Jesus Christ is the same yesterday, today, and forever.

— Hebrews 13:8 (NKJV)

In one sense, it's easy to describe the qualities of the Lord Jesus Christ: They are almost the same as those of our Heavenly Father. We only see minor differences here and there. For example, Jesus is in heaven with a glorified body. Because He in no way usurps the role of our Heavenly Father, His relationship to us as saved people is as our sibling (Matthew 12:50, NKJV). In the same way that our Heavenly Father is our perfect father, Jesus is also a perfect sibling.

Jesus is also timeless. His existence predates the creation because all of that occurred through Him. In fact, He holds all things together now so that everything continues to exist. He also rules our lives through having all authority in heaven and on Earth.

Because while on Earth Jesus was completely human, as well as completely God, He knows what it is to be human at a very fundamental level. Because of that experience, He is happy to have us speak candidly to Him about whatever troubles our hearts, souls, spirits, and minds.

It's easy for us to feel a bit differently about Jesus than we feel about our Heavenly Father due to appreciating the incredible sacrifice that Jesus made on the way to and on the cross so that we could come to life spiritually and be with our Heavenly Father, Him, and the Holy Spirit for all eternity. Many people will ascribe much of their love for Jesus to His having paid this terrible price to redeem us from our sins.

If you found it easier through the prior lesson to want to draw closer to our Heavenly Father in love, surely you feel at least as much of the same desire now to do so with our Lord and Savior, Jesus Christ.

Draw Closer to Our Heavenly Father, the Lord Jesus Christ, and the Holy Spirit by Learning the Qualities of the Lord Jesus Christ

Many people have somewhat similar understandings of the qualities of the Lord Jesus Christ. Based on how we came to faith in Him, however, we may have quite different perceptions of what kind of relationship it is possible to have with Him. For some, Jesus can be a remote figure, rather than a much loved and loving sibling. For others, His perfection can be so intimidating that they feel most comfortable watching Him from afar. As a result of perceiving different relationship possibilities, many believers experience quite different degrees of closeness to Him. Regardless of where your relationship with Him is now, Jesus wants to be closer to you. The following questions are designed to help you play your part in making that happen after experiencing and appreciating Him more completely:

1. As you read the verses in this lesson, what aspects of the qualities of God's Son Jesus were new to you?

2. How does considering those qualities change your desire to experience Him more fully?

3. As you read those same verses, were there any aspects of the Lord Jesus Christ that struck you as being more important?

4. If yes, how does sensing greater importance for those qualities affect how you think about and feel towards Him?

5. How can you more completely relate to Him as your Lord, Savior, and sibling?

6. What would you like to say to Jesus now, for the first time?

7. How did what you said change how close you feel to Him?

8. What can you do differently today to increase your awareness of His presence?

9. How did those changes affect your closeness to Him?

10. How will you draw still closer to Him in the future?

Week One Memory Verse

"Every good gift and every perfect gift is from above, and comes down from the Father of lights, …." (James 1:17, NKJV)

Week One: Days Five and Six

Learn the Qualities of the Holy Spirit

In the beginning God created the heavens and the earth.
The earth was without form, and void;
and darkness was on the face of the deep.
And the Spirit of God was hovering over the face of the waters.

— Genesis 1:1-2 (NKJV)

"But the Helper, the Holy Spirit,
whom the Father will send in My name,
He will teach you all things, and
bring to your remembrance all things that I said to you."

— John 14:26 (NKJV)

"However, when He, the Spirit of truth, has come,
He will guide you into all truth;
for He will not speak on His own authority,
but whatever He hears He will speak;
and He will tell you things to come.
He will glorify Me, for He will
take of what is Mine and declare it to you.
All things that the Father has are Mine.
Therefore I said that He will take of Mine
and declare it to you."

— John 16:13-15 (NKJV)

"But you shall receive power
when the Holy Spirit has come upon you;
and you shall be witnesses to Me in Jerusalem,
and in all Judea and Samaria,
and to the end of the earth."

— Acts 1:8 (NKJV)

But the manifestation of the Spirit is given to each one
for the profit of all: for to one is given the word of wisdom
through the Spirit, to another the word of knowledge
through the same Spirit, to another faith by the same Spirit,
to another gifts of healings by the same Spirit,
to another the working of miracles, to another prophecy,
to another discerning of spirits,
to another different kinds of tongues,
to another the interpretation of tongues.
But one and the same Spirit works all these things,
distributing to each one individually as He wills.

— 1 Corinthians 12:7-11 (NKJV)

Likewise the Spirit also helps in our weaknesses.
For we do not know what we should pray for as we ought,
But the Spirit Himself makes intercession for us
with groanings which cannot be uttered.

— Romans 8:26 (NKJV)

New Testament references to the Holy Spirit are few in number. In considering the ones we have, it's good to start by remembering that the Holy Spirit was present as the heavens and Earth were created. As our prior lesson reminded us, the Holy Spirit was also part of the process by which Jesus came to be born of Mary.

We are reminded that spiritual beings can be persons, as we see when Jesus refers to the Holy Spirit as "He" in John 14:26 (NKJV). That kind of reference is repeated by Jesus in John 16:13-16 (NKJV), providing added proof for anyone who thinks that the first such reference might be a fluke.

So what is the role of the Holy Spirit? We would have to include many Old Testament references to be fully detailed, but the verses in this and the prior lesson make it clear that the Holy Spirit brings Godly communications (such as by reminding us of what Jesus said and by praying on our behalf with "groanings"), guidance towards the truth, as well as spiritual power (especially by providing spiritual gifts for accomplishing the tasks of God's Kingdom).

The Holy Spirit can be inside or outside of us. Before we become believers, the Holy Spirit is external to us. As Jesus' words and the events of Pentecost demonstrate, believers have the Holy Spirit within them, helping to propel the sanctification process by which each believer gradually becomes more like Jesus. The Holy Spirit does so by affecting our hearts, abilities, and personalities. Consequently, as believers we have already been intimately affected by the closeness of the Holy Spirit.

Because of the unique roles of the Holy Spirit and His help, it's easy for a believer to communicate to our Heavenly Father and the Lord Jesus Christ, yet not attempt to draw closer to the Holy Spirit Himself. So we have the paradoxical situation of perhaps ignoring the Holy Spirit, in part due to how well He does His work. When such a situation is the case, we may have more ground to cover for drawing closer to the Holy Spirit than to either our Heavenly Father or the Lord Jesus Christ.

Draw Closer to Our Heavenly Father, the Lord Jesus Christ, and the Holy Spirit by Learning the Qualities of the Holy Spirit

Many people have limited understandings of the qualities of the Holy Spirit. Believers vary even more in terms of how much they have thought about the Holy Spirit, and what kind of relationship is possible and desirable to have with Him. Regardless of the understanding and kind of relationship you have now, the Holy Spirit wants to be closer to you. The following questions are designed to help you make progress in this regard through experiencing and appreciating Him more completely:

1. As you read the verses that begin this lesson, what aspects of the qualities of the Holy Spirit were new to you?

2. How does considering those qualities change your desire to experience Him more fully?

3. As you read those same verses, did any aspects of the Holy Spirit strike you as being more important?

4. If yes, how does sensing greater importance for these qualities affect how you think and feel about Him?

5. How can you more completely relate to Him as your source of Godly communications, guidance towards the truth, and spiritual power?

6. Do you ask to be refilled with the Holy Spirit when you speak to our Heavenly Father and the Lord Jesus Christ?

7. What would you like to say to the Holy Spirit now, for the first time?

8. How did what you said change how close you feel to Him?

9. What can you do differently today to increase your awareness of His presence?

10. How did those changes affect your closeness to Him?

11. How will you conduct your life differently due to better understanding the qualities of the Holy Spirit?

Week One Memory Verse

"Every good gift and every perfect gift is from above, and comes down from
the Father of lights, ..." (James 1:17, NKJV)

Week Two: Days One and Two

Spend More Time in Prayer

Now in the morning, having risen a long while before daylight,
He went out and departed to a solitary place; and there He prayed.

— Mark 1:35 (NKJV)

And when He had sent the multitudes away,
He went up on the mountain by Himself to pray.
Now when evening came, He was alone there.

— Matthew 14:23 (NKJV)

Now it came to pass in those days
that He went out to the mountain to pray, and
continued all night in prayer to God.

— Luke 6:12 (NKJV)

Then the disciples came to Jesus privately and said,
"Why could we not cast it out?"

So Jesus said to them,
"Because of your unbelief; for assuredly, I say to you,
if you have faith as a mustard seed,
you will say to this mountain,
'Move from here to there,' and it will move;
and nothing will be impossible for you.
However, this kind does not go out except by prayer and fasting."

— Matthew 17:19-21 (NKJV)

Then little children were brought to Him
that He might put His hands on them and pray,
but the disciples rebuked them.

— Matthew 19:13 (NKJV)

Then Jesus came with them to a place called Gethsemane,
and said to the disciples,
"Sit here while I go and pray over there."

— Matthew 26:36 (NKJV)

Many believers are unaware of how much time they spend in prayer. If you say only a short version of grace over three meals daily, the combined length could be as little as 90 seconds ... or perhaps even less than that. Some people don't even do that much praying each day. Even some full-time pastors report spending relatively little time in prayer.

If we simply consider what Jesus did in this regard, we can see that such limited time in prayer might not be the best practice. When Jesus was facing major decisions, such as choosing the twelve apostles, He engaged in extended prayer alone, as Luke 6:12 (NKJV) tells us. We also know that He prayed for hours at Gethsemane before the trials of His betrayal and subsequent crucifixion, while the apostles slept nearby. Surely, we need to pray even more than Jesus did while He was here on Earth.

We can see another useful example of extended prayer in the life of Anna, who was given the great honor of helping to proclaim the significance of Jesus' birth when He was brought to the Temple to be presented:

Now there was one, Anna, a prophetess, the daughter of Phanuel, of the tribe of Asher. She was of a great age, and had lived with a husband seven years from her virginity; and this woman *was* a widow of about eighty-four years, who did not depart from the temple, but served *God* with fastings and prayers night and day. And coming in that instant she gave thanks to the Lord, and spoke of Him to all those who looked for redemption in Jerusalem. (Luke 2:36-38, NKJV)

Clearly, longer amounts of time in prayer are needed to develop and maintain the right relationship with God, as well as to prepare for doing the most important tasks for Him and the Kingdom. As demonstrated by the examples of Jesus being able to cast out a certain kind of demon and of Anna preparing for her big moment in serving God, fasting may also be helpful for focusing attention to make prayer more effective.

If you truly love God and want to fulfill your purpose for Him, shouldn't you be in longer conversations listening to and speaking with Him?

Draw Closer to Our Heavenly Father, the Lord Jesus Christ, and the Holy Spirit by Spending More Time in Prayer

A good starting point for beginning to spend more time is prayer is to become more aware of how much time you do so now, both alone and with others. If you perceive that amount of time is quite brief, your heart will probably lead you to increase the amount of time so devoted. Even if too much brevity is not the case, consider how adding prayer time can be a spiritual adventure that will probably help improve your relationship with God. However, only increase time spent in prayer because you love God and enjoy spending time listening to and speaking with Him ... rather than as a way to try to "score points" with Him. As you increase the time you spend, set no objectives and don't keep track of time while you are praying, but rather focus more on simply being with Him as you are. The following questions are designed to help guide your heart in choosing what to do while spending more daily time in prayer:

1. What do you appreciate about God that you have not been praising Him for during your prayers?

2. What are you not thanking God for during your prayers?

3. Who do you need to ask God to help you forgive?

4. What sins are you not admitting to God in prayer?

5. What sins are you not repenting and asking for His help to turn away from repeating during your prayers?

6. Of what important promises that God has made are you not reminding Him while praying?

7. What examples from the Bible are you citing or asking questions about in your prayers?

8. What commands are you asking God to help you obey through your prayers?

9. What truths are you acknowledging in prayer that God has described?

10. What prayer requests are you making to God so that you can do more for His Kingdom?

11. What prayer requests are you making to God so that others can do more for His Kingdom?

12. How are you using your prayers to become more humble in listening to and speaking with God?

13. How well are you listening to Him before and after you speak in prayer?

14. What matters are you not discussing with Him?

15. How often are you praying aloud?

16. How can you expand and improve your relationship with God through changing your prayer life?

Week Two Memory Verse

"Watch and pray, lest you enter into temptation. The spirit indeed *is* willing, but the flesh *is* weak." (Matthew 26:41, NKJV)

Week Two: Days Three and Four

Pray More Often

"And whatever things you ask in prayer, believing,
you will receive."

— Matthew 21:22 (NKJV)

Rejoice always, pray without ceasing,
in everything give thanks;
for this is the will of God in Christ Jesus for you.

— 1 Thessalonians 5:16-18 (NKJV)

Many believers find the direction to "pray without ceasing" to be one of the more challenging and puzzling in the Bible. If you are one of such people, relax. Think of what is indicated as simply meaning that you should be continually aware of God's presence and listening for or speaking with Him as you would with any other highly esteemed, nearby companion.

Consider as a contrast the prayer life of a believer who focuses almost all of his or her attention on God during Sunday services, church events, and at times of sudden crisis. Such an individual will often be walling God off from her or his consciousness the rest of the time, especially while focusing on things that seem, at least on the surface, to be merely secular.

Keep in mind that there are two aspects to prayer: *listening and speaking.* Praying without ceasing means, in part, always expecting that God might be sending you a message. In other words, you are always paying attention to what He might want to share with you. If He doesn't speak or send a message, you might, instead, initiate a conversation by praising and thanking Him, commenting on something good He has done, repenting, asking forgiveness, or making requests; however, you should remember that He could interrupt or direct you at any time in some nonverbal way. In this manner, you will be actively present with Him whenever you are awake.

Matthew 21:22 (NKJV) introduces two important benefits of praying without ceasing: building your faith and accomplishing more for God's Kingdom. Jesus told us that we will receive whatever we pray for while having full belief in its fulfillment. Having such belief requires help from the Holy Spirit. Having such faith, you'll make more requests, especially more requests that fit with God's plans for you and His Kingdom. Doing so will permit God to grant you more opportunities and resources so that you can accomplish more in His name. What could be finer?

So what should you ask for? Well, some believers make the mistake of thinking that God only wants to deal with the very biggest issues. However, He is just as interested in the little things that can enable you to draw closer to Him and accomplish more for the Kingdom. We see such interest in how God takes care of the birds and counts the hairs on our heads. It's also easy for us to underestimate the importance of what seems little to us. In God's eyes, a tiny thing might be like a mustard seed that can become a mighty influence for good. With this expanded view of His interests, you might ask for a closer parking place so that you'll have enough time to share your testimony with someone before starting your next activity. Why wouldn't He want to hear from and help you with that request?

Every conversation doesn't need to include a request. After all, He isn't Santa, and you aren't a small child sitting on His knee just before Christmas with a list of toys you want. In fact, your joy will often be increased more by simply telling Him how much you love Him than by making any requests and receiving what you asked for.

Draw Closer to Our Heavenly Father, the Lord Jesus Christ, and the Holy Spirit through More Often Praying

Increasing the frequency of their prayers is difficult for some believers. A good way to overcome any challenges in this regard is by developing new habits that direct your mind to God, both to listen to Him and to share what's in your heart with Him, when certain situations and events occur. Here are some questions to help you get started in identifying what situations and events could remind you to draw closer to Him through more frequent prayer:

1. When something good happens to you, do you stop to appreciate that God provided it and to thank Him?

2. When something that seems to be bad happens to you, do you thank Him, as well?

3. When don't you listen for what God has to say to you?

4. Why don't you listen then?

5. What would you have to change to hear and respond to Him at such times?

6. For what kinds of things do you seek God's guidance?

7. For what kinds of things do you not ask for His guidance?

8. Do you always speak to God when you feel lonely?

9. If you don't speak to God at such times, why don't you?

10. If you have a bad day, does that cause you to pray to God more? Or do you pray less?

11. What annoyances do you never take to God?

12. What do you have hopes for that you haven't talked to God about?

13. Are there times of the day when you never speak to God?

14. How could you begin speaking to Him then?

15. What will you do differently to pray to God much more often today … and tomorrow?

16. How did you feel after praying to God more often today?

Week Two Memory Verse

"Watch and pray, lest you enter into temptation. The spirit indeed *is* willing, but the flesh *is* weak."
(Matthew 26:41, NKJV)

Week Two: Days Five and Six

Pray More Effectively

"And when you pray, you shall not be like the hypocrites.
For they love to pray standing in the synagogues and
on the corners of the streets, that they may be seen by men.
Assuredly, I say to you, they have their reward.
But you, when you pray, go into your room,
and when you have shut your door,
pray to your Father who is in the secret place; and
your Father who sees in secret will reward you openly.
And when you pray, do not use
vain repetitions as the heathen do.
For they think that they will be heard for their many words.

"Therefore do not be like them.
For your Father knows the things
you have need of before you ask Him.
In this manner, therefore, pray:

Our Father in heaven,
Hallowed be Your name.
Your kingdom come.
Your will be done
On earth as it is in heaven.
Give us this day our daily bread.
And forgive us our debts,
As we forgive our debtors.
And do not lead us into temptation,
But deliver us from the evil one.
For Yours is the kingdom and the power
and the glory forever. Amen.

"For if you forgive men their trespasses,
your heavenly Father will also forgive you.
But if you do not forgive men their trespasses,
neither will your Father forgive your trespasses."

— Matthew 6:5-15 (NKJV)

Many believers find praying to be very difficult, especially if asked to pray aloud. Yet, Jesus clearly explained how to pray, even providing a model of what the elements of a prayer should be.

Let's take Matthew 6:5-15 (NKJV) as a foundation to build on for praying more effectively. First, notice that there's a precondition in the model prayer: Before we ask for our debts (falling short of acting righteously in all things, including any wrongs we have done others) to be forgiven, we must have already forgiven those who owe us such debts. To be sure we don't miss the point, Jesus specifically talked about the same being true of *trespasses* at the end of these verses.

Does everyone forgive all others for their wrongs done to them before praying to God? Perhaps such forgiveness is always granted. Whether or not it is, forgiveness should precede prayer. If you don't already forgive everyone in this way, you can start doing so today.

Second, we should usually pray in private when that's an option. Jesus clearly followed that prescription on the occasions when He retreated for long prayer sessions with His Heavenly Father.

Third, however we pray, we should be sure to do so with only God in mind, rather than trying to make an impression on other people.

Fourth, while it's fine to keep asking God to fill the same need in our prayers, we shouldn't be doing so repeatedly in the same prayer. Praying is a conversation with God, not a broadcast or a mantra.

Fifth, we should praise God for His wonderful qualities and what He has done for us. Doing so helps us reach the proper state of humility, as we contemplate the vast differences between God and us.

Sixth, we should be praying for His will to be done and His Kingdom to come on Earth. Some believers do not appear to fully understand this point. We are here to serve God and His Kingdom. When we request help that enables His will to be done and His Kingdom to come, we are fitting in with His program. However, many people disconnect what they think about, want, and request from seeking to serve His purposes. Instead, some believers might ask for help and for things that fail to coincide with (or, worst of all, might oppose) His will and plans for the Kingdom. That's a big mistake!

The other elements of the model prayer are pretty straightforward, so no more need be said on those points. However, here's one final thought: This is a *model* for a prayer … not the actual prayer that we should always use. Would you *always* say exactly the same thing to your boss, your neighbor, and your best friend? Of course, you would not do so.

Keep all these elements in mind as topics to bring into your prayers. As you do, speak directly to God in a way that reflects and builds on the relationship you have with Him.

Of course, your prayers aren't limited just to doing these things. You can also add elements that are more specific to helping you act in accord with what your prayer says, such as by requesting to be refilled with the Holy Spirit or to notice God's intentions more often.

As you pray more effectively, your sense of being in God's presence is sure to increase and feel more rewarding. How great that will be!

Draw Closer to Our Heavenly Father, the Lord Jesus Christ, and the Holy Spirit by Praying More Effectively

Anyone can learn to pray more effectively. Consequently, this lesson can make a big difference in your relationship with God if you haven't been following all of what Jesus said in Matthew 6:5-15 (NKJV). The following questions are designed to help you identify any ways you can improve your prayers:

1. Do you always forgive others for whatever they have done to you before praying?

2. If you don't always do so, how can you change your practices so that you will?

3. Do you pray in private as often as possible?

4. If not, how could you do so more often?

5. Are you totally focused on God as you pray?

6. If not, how could you more totally focus on Him?

7. Are you praising God and thanking Him for what He has done in every prayer?

8. If not, how can you always do so in the future?

9. Do you always confess your unrepented sins, turn away from doing them again, and ask God for forgiveness when you speak to Him?

10. If not, how can you be sure to do so?

11. Do you use Jesus' model prayer as directions for prayer content, rather than always repeating it verbatim?

12. If not, how can you shift to speaking more personally and specifically to God?

13. Are all your prayer requests aimed at advancing His will and His Kingdom?

14. If not, how should you change what you pray for and how you ask for what you request?

15. What are you leaving out of your prayers that you should include?

16. How can you make the most effective prayer you have ever made to God right now?

17. How do you feel differently now that you've made that prayer?

18. Are you attentive to how God might respond to your prayers?

19. If not, how could you increase your awareness of His responses and actions?

20. How will you pray differently from now on?

Week Two Memory Verse

"Watch and pray, lest you enter into temptation. The spirit indeed *is* willing, but the flesh *is* weak."
(Matthew 26:41, NKJV)

Week Three: Days One and Two

Develop and Follow a Bible-Study Routine

But He said,
"More than that, blessed are *those who*
hear the word of God and keep it!"

— Luke 11:28 (NKJV)

Resist the devil and he will flee from you.

— James 4:7 (NKJV)

Many believers describe their lives as burdensome whenever they deal with challenges beyond their personal abilities and resources to solve. Yet in many cases, the Bible describes a good solution for such difficulties, a solution that the believers are unaware of or have forgotten exists. What's missing here? Such individuals would benefit from a Bible-study routine that includes checking to see what the Bible has to say about whatever is going on in their lives. For example, when Jesus was tempted by the devil while in the wilderness, He quickly got rid of the tempter by quoting Scripture. We can do the same. With today's easy access to multiple translations of the Bible connected to key-word-search capabilities, even the newest believer should be able to quickly find relevant guidance in God's Word.

As more knowledge of the Bible develops, new kinds of questions will arise in a believer's mind. In many cases, these questions will involve reconciling different statements in the Bible that don't at first seem to be in accord with one another. In such cases, deeper Bible study will be required, one that may involve looking into what various words meant in the original languages of that time (Hebrew, Greek, or Aramaic). Beyond that, it may be useful to read commentaries describing the meanings of the apparently conflicting passages. In some few cases, it may be necessary to share the question with a pastor. However, if the answer isn't sought, faith may be reduced. Since God wants to perfect our faith, we should do our part by praying for His help with understanding His will while doing what we can with the resources He has provided. Such prayers should be part of a good Bible-study routine.

Each believer will live a more fruitful life if he or she also learns more about what the Bible says, what Jesus commanded, and how we are to conduct our lives. Doing so will often reveal areas of life where sinning is occurring due to ignorance of what God wants. Surely, a Bible-study routine should seek to eliminate any such ignorance. To do so, it's a good practice to read the Bible from cover to cover in several different translations. Using online resources, there's no cost to do so on your electronic device beyond some electricity.

Once you have a favorite translation, you may also want to mark up a printed copy with the key points you learn as you go. Then you will be able to more quickly understand verses when they are referenced in sermons and during Bible discussions.

You may have other needs that can be addressed through Bible study. Regardless of what such needs are, find a way to address them as part of your routine.

Be sure that your Bible-study routine *always* includes daily time spent reading, meditating on, and applying the Bible. As you do, keep an eye open for any sins that you didn't realize you were committing, Biblical principles that you should follow, examples that can guide you (such as Jesus in the wilderness), God's commands to obey, God's promises, and all statements of truth about God and His Kingdom that you can base your faith on and mention in your prayers.

Draw Closer to Our Heavenly Father, the Lord Jesus Christ, and the Holy Spirit by Developing and Following a Bible-Study Routine

Even if you already have a daily Bible-study routine, it's a good idea to examine how well that routine enables you to experience God. You should pray for guidance in this regard and try different approaches. Here are some questions intended to help you develop or improve a Bible-study routine:

1. How do you use the Bible now to find solutions to difficulties and challenges you face?

2. How could a Bible-study routine help you to do so more effectively and often?

3. How do you reconcile verses that seem to be in conflict when you encounter them?

4. How could a Bible-study routine help you to do so more effectively and often?

5. How do you expand your knowledge of what the whole Bible says?

6. How could a Bible-study routine help you to do so more effectively and often?

7. How do you quickly develop accurate perspectives on a verse that someone mentions in a sermon or in a Bible study?

8. How could a Bible-study routine help you to do so more effectively and often?

9. What other needs do you have for Bible-based knowledge and wisdom?

10. How could a Bible-study routine help you to gain such knowledge and wisdom more effectively and often?

11. What should your Bible-study routine include each day?

12. When should you engage in that routine today?

13. How did it feel to engage in this routine for the first time?

14. What benefits do you feel you will gain from continuing?

Week Three Memory Verse

"Resist the devil and he will flee from you." (James 4:7, NKJV)

Week Three: Days Three and Four

Develop and Follow a Bible-Study Curriculum

Now so it was that *after three days*
they found Him in the temple,
sitting in the midst of the teachers,
both listening to them and asking them questions.

— Luke 2:46 (NKJV)

For the word of God is *living and powerful, and*
sharper than any two-edged sword,
piercing even to the division of soul and spirit,
and of joints and marrow, and
is a discerner of the thoughts and intents of the heart.

— Hebrews 4:12 (NKJV)

In Luke 2:46 (NKJV), we learn what drew the boy Jesus to remain in the Temple in Jerusalem after His parents had headed home, thus causing them a great scare: Jesus wanted to learn from the teachers there, both by listening and asking questions. In those days, the only copies of the Old Testament existed on hand-produced scrolls that were very expensive. Since the Temple had more scrolls than most other places, it was an unusually good place to study such materials, providing the teachers there with the opportunity to develop more insights than teachers who studied elsewhere. In Hebrews 4:12 (NKJV), we also see a remarkable presentation of why understanding the Bible is so critical: The Bible is a living and powerful tool from God that can probe deep within us to show us the truth and to discern the righteousness of our thoughts and intentions.

Much as Jesus wanted to gain the most knowledge by spending time with teachers at the Temple, believers should seek to gain as much knowledge of the whole Bible as possible, especially with relation to understanding Jesus' commands in the New Testament. Be cautious as you do so. Some believers totally ignore the Old Testament, failing by doing so to appreciate what that part of the Bible teaches. As an example of why this is a mistake, notice how often Jesus referred to and quoted Old Testament verses.

A curriculum simply covers all the topics necessary for understanding a subject. In considering this task, be sure that your Bible studies will provide you with a broad and a deep knowledge of God and His will.

Since everyone starts at a different point in seeking such knowledge, let me simply describe some of the elements that can be helpful to include in a Bible-study curriculum:

1. *Read the Bible in at least five different translations involving a variety of methods.* Some translations emphasize being literal in replicating language, while others focus on fitting the meaning to a current context, and still others make adjustments somewhere between those two dimensions (such as by using today's language and making

some contextual adjustments). You will learn more if you read all three kinds of translations. You may also find it helpful to read the same verses in all the translations at the same time, enabling you to gain a more comprehensive sense of what all the translations are pointing towards.

2. *Listen to different teachers who discuss verses in different translations.* Many pastors record verse-by-verse, chapter-by-chapter sermons that are available online. You will find the background information provided in some of such teachings to be very useful for expanding your understanding. However, don't expect all such pastors to agree on the meaning. If you aren't sure which recordings to use for this purpose, ask your pastor for suggestions of whom to listen to for this purpose.

3. *Read Bible commentaries.* Many of such commentaries also go verse-by-verse and chapter-by-chapter to discuss the Bible's contents. These resources often contain helpful background material, as well. Since few libraries carry such books, you may have to purchase or borrow such commentaries.

Fit your curriculum to your Bible-study routine so that your learning becomes more efficient. For instance, if you read some verses one day, you might then listen to teachers discuss the same verses the next day, and shift to reading commentaries concerning the verses on the third day. Or, if you prefer, you could read the commentaries before listening to the teachers. Try both sequences to see which order of study works better for you.

Draw Closer to Our Heavenly Father, the Lord Jesus Christ, and the Holy Spirit by Developing and Following a Bible-Study Curriculum

Even if you have been studying the Bible for many years, you may have gaps in understanding due to how you have done so. Consider how improvements might be made so that you can better experience God. You should pray for guidance and examine what you have been doing to make improvements. Here are some questions intended to help you either develop or improve a Bible-study curriculum:

1. What types of translations have you used in your Bible study?

2. What types would be good to add?

3. What teachers have you listened to concerning Bible verses?

4. How could listening to other teachers increase your knowledge?

5. What commentaries about Bible verses, chapters, and books do you read now?

6. What other commentaries might expand your understanding and help you experience God more fully?

7. What does answering the prior six questions tell you about how complete your Bible-study curriculum has been for enabling you to draw closer to our Heavenly Father, the Lord Jesus Christ, and the Holy Spirit?

8. What will you do differently to draw closer to Them through a better Bible-study curriculum?

9. How did doing so enable you to draw closer to Them?

<u>Week Three Memory Verse</u>

"Resist the devil and he will flee from you." (James 4:7, NKJV)

Week Three: Days Five and Six

Use Bible Study to Seek Answers to Challenges

But He answered and said,
"It is written, 'Man shall not live by bread alone,
but by every word that proceeds from the mouth of God.'"

— Matthew 4:4 (NKJV)

Matthew 4:4 (NKJV) tells us that what God says and has said is as fundamental as food for our lives. In the same way that most people concentrate their eating during a few times of the day, Bible study is concentrated by most people into a single time daily and into a predetermined program, an approach the prior lesson encouraged you to apply.

However, there's more to be usefully done. Imagine if you only did something about fire prevention after a harmful fire in your home. Wouldn't that be pretty silly? With such an approach, you wouldn't eliminate the most common causes of such fires until it was too late to benefit.

When a challenge comes your way, God intends for you to use the Bible as part of receiving directions for what should be done and how to do it. In the same way that you would pick up a phone to call the fire department for help with putting out a fire, you should pick up your Bible when you notice a challenge of any kind that faces you or those you love.

Unless you have been thoroughly studying the Bible from many perspectives over a long period of time, chances are that you won't know where to turn in the Bible for guidance concerning a new kind of challenge. If that's the case, look up words that relate to the challenge that might appear in a Bible index, either online or in print.

Should that kind of searching not help sufficiently, seek guidance from a pastor at your church about what portions of the Bible to study, think and pray about, and apply. You might also look for believers who have grappled with such challenges and can provide useful suggestions. Some of such believers may be involved in groups that regularly address such challenges, and you might be able to join in them for directed Bible study, prayer, and mutual encouragement.

Stop relying solely on your own thinking in deciding what to do. When you take such a narrow approach, you will miss an opportunity to draw closer to God, and you may be less fruitful than He intends for you to be with the spiritual gifts and other resources He has given you to address such a challenge. For example, after having received God's great help in defeating Jericho, Joshua failed to seek God's direction for engaging with Ai. Consequently, the Israelites suffered an embarrassing defeat as their warriors turned their backs on the enemy and fled. Only after the Israelites cleansed themselves of unrighteousness at God's direction did He again take the lead in their battles. Stay with His plan!

Draw Closer to Our Heavenly Father, the Lord Jesus Christ, and the Holy Spirit by Using Bible Study to Seek Answers to Challenges

Particularly when you face a new challenge, your past Bible studies may prove inadequate for informing you about what to do. You could also feel so overwhelmed by the challenge that you start trying to deal with it before finding out what God has said and is saying on the subject. The following questions are designed to make you more aware of the need for special Bible study and direct you in conducting it:

1. What types of challenges have you already used Bible study to address?

2. What types of Bible study would be good to add so that you will be prepared for other challenges should they occur?

3. What can remind you to immediately seek answers in the Bible to any new challenges?

4. How can you use your knowledge to gain more answers from the Bible to your new challenges?

5. What other resources might help you locate the relevant parts of the Bible and better understand their applications to the challenge?

6. Who can guide you to still other resources?

7. What kinds of challenges have you dealt with in the past without the Bible's guidance?

8. What could you do differently now to avoid repeating such excessive self-reliance?

9. What promise of God's will make you seek His Word first when you face your next new challenge?

10. What lessons do you want to apply from your past experiences while doing so?

11. What challenge will you investigate today with the Bible's guidance?

12. How does it make you feel to begin looking for answers to challenges you haven't yet faced?

13. How does seeing the Bible as always being a resource for dealing with challenges change your view of the relationship you should have with God?

Week Three Memory Verse

"Resist the devil and he will flee from you." (James 4:7, NKJV)

Week Four: Days One and Two

Track Your Prayer Requests

"Ask, and it will be given to you; seek, and you will find;
knock, and it will be opened to you.
For everyone who asks receives, and he who seeks finds, and
to him who knocks it will be opened.
Or what man is there among you who,
if his son asks for bread, will give him a stone?
Or if he asks for a fish, will he give him a serpent?
If you then, being evil,
know how to give good gifts to your children,
how much more will your Father who is in heaven
give good things to those who ask Him!"

— Matthew 7:7-11 (NKJV)

On days five and six of week one and days one and two of week two in Part One, you listed and thought about your prayer requests that God has fulfilled, as well as the possible benefits of His not choosing to fulfill other prayers. If you haven't already begun a prayer journal, now is the time to do so.

I have been making notes about my prayers for many years in a hardbound journal. It is pretty well worn from use, but the binding and pages have held up well enough so that I can review what I have prayed for and what ensued.

I strongly urge you to find a similarly sturdy notebook so that many years from now your notes will still be bound together in the correct order, allowing you to review your prayerful interactions with God. If you are like me, simply writing your prayer requests will probably encourage you to make more of them. So be sure to obtain a big notebook!

Some people may prefer to create an electronic version of such requests. While that's quite good for the short term, I find that many of my electronic documents end up disappearing whenever I change computers or electronic devices. Such a loss would be a shame. A big notebook that you look at every day is harder to lose or ignore.

While one obvious benefit of writing your prayers is for you to become more aware of what God did with the requests, another valuable benefit may not have occurred to you: The list of what you are praying for now will remind you to keep praying in faith for anything about which God hasn't yet responded.

I love to pray, and everyone who knows me appreciates this preference of mine. As a result, I receive a lot of prayer requests. I immediately begin to pray for results when it is obvious that they will improve or expand God's Kingdom. When I'm not sure about that connection, I ask for more information from the person who made the request, check the Bible for relevance, and ask God if He wants me to pray in this way.

However, in the course of being so engaged, it's easy for me to lose track of something that I intend to pray for. Mostly this forgetting occurs when someone interrupts my morning quiet time or my schedule becomes so overly full that my morning prayer time is temporarily curtailed. When I again have enough time to pray as long as I want, it's easy for me to forget something I had intended to pray for unless my list reminds me to do so.

It's good to not only have such a list, but also to date when you began and ended various prayers. Doing so will give you a better sense of what God's timing often looks like for addressing various kinds of needs. I also find that looking at the dates helps me appreciate more about my spiritual development at that point in my life.

If you don't have time to obtain a notebook today, write down your prayers anyway ... and transfer what you wrote into the notebook after you obtain it. Realizing that you are making extra work for yourself may encourage you to get the notebook sooner!

Draw Closer to Our Heavenly Father, the Lord Jesus Christ, and the Holy Spirit by Tracking Your Prayer Requests

As this lesson suggests, your faith can be aided by creating a record of your prayers to remind you what to keep praying for so that Godly purposes will come to fruition. In addition, using this record in various ways will also encourage you to pray for more ways to expand and improve God's Kingdom. The following questions are designed to help you get off to a good start:

1. Do you write down the prayers you have made?

2. If so, how do you use what you have written?

3. How would it help you to record your prayers more systematically and thoroughly?

4. How could your prayers be enhanced by doing so?

5. What could such changes do for your faith?

6. What would be the best way for you to make such a record so that it would be of use to you for many years to come?

7. How did you pray differently as a result of tracking all of your prayer requests?

8. Who else might be able to use what you record?

9. How does it make you feel to treat your prayer requests more seriously?

10. How can you be sure to maintain such tracking?

Week Four Memory Verse

"Ask, and it will be given to you; seek, and you will find; knock, and it will be opened to you."
(Matthew 7:7, NKJV)

Week Four: Days Three and Four

Record Answers to Your Prayer Requests

"He who is of God hears God's words;
therefore you do not hear,
because you are not of God."

— John 8:47 (NKJV)

For some believers, the idea of receiving answers to prayer requests, separate from those requests being perfectly fulfilled, seems like a strange notion. After all, perhaps such a person has never heard God's voice, run into a Bible verse that responded to a prayer request, encountered circumstances that blocked or eased the route to a request being fulfilled, or had a strong feeling that a request would be or would not be fulfilled ... now or in the future. For such a person, this lesson might present special challenges and great opportunities for spiritual development.

To help with any possible confusion about God's answers to prayers, let me discuss some ways that God can choose to do so. First, if you have been praying for something for many years and it hasn't happened yet, you can probably assume that God's answer to your prayer so far has been either "not now" or "no." How, then, might you distinguish between those two possible answers? Well, consider if there's a free-will act required by someone else for the prayer to be fulfilled. If that's the case and the result would unquestionably be good for God's Kingdom, then the answer is probably "not now." For instance, you might have prayed for a child to come to faith. Well, the child has to repent and accept Jesus for that blessed result to occur. God won't force the child to make that decision, but He will present circumstances and messages that will encourage the child. If you see such circumstances and messages occurring in a child's life, then you can probably assume that God's answer was "I'm working on it," rather than "not now" or "no."

Second, some changes related to what is being prayed for might occur almost immediately. Such changes might not precisely match what you prayed for, but they might address at least one aspect of your request. As an example, I often pray for those who tailgate (follow too closely) my car not to hit me or anyone else, and for them to arrive safely. After I pray, the other driver almost always drops back to a reasonable stopping distance behind my car. A few of them will safely pass me instead. I believe in either case that God has answered "yes" to my prayer, even if I never see that person arrive safely at a final destination.

Third, I am often on a mailing list of those requesting prayers. Such a letter or e-mail usually spells out what kind of prayer is desired and for what purposes. If someone lets me know what subsequently happens, I can possibly use that knowledge to understand God's answer. In such cases, it's not unusual for God to provide a solution vastly different from what I specifically prayed for, but one which, in part, fulfills the same purpose. In other cases, I'll see something in the news that provides the answer, even if I never hear again from the person who requested the prayer. Or, I might see a post on a social-media site from the person whom I wanted to be spared from the ravages of a storm, allowing me to infer that he or she must have been so blessed.

Fourth, the Holy Spirit sometimes floods me with an immediate sense of peace after I pray for something specific. From reviewing the ensuing results, I have noticed that such peace has often followed either a "yes" or a "no" answer to my prayer. While experiencing such peace, I might then receive a strong impulse to check on something. Doing so will usually reveal that God will or will not grant the request.

Fifth, sometimes I have no idea what the answer is. In those cases, I pray for clarity in this regard. After doing so, I am often pointed to a Bible verse in a sermon, a commentary, or an e-mail that seems to directly respond to my issue. I then think about the Bible verse or other information source and ask God if I'm interpreting it correctly. If I feel peaceful at that point, I conclude that I have done so.

You have probably had your own experiences with learning God's answers. I encourage you to use those experiences as guideposts to help you identify future answers, as well. I make this observation because I assume that I initially miss answers that God has sent. I make that assumption based on the number of times that I've noticed multiple indications of the answer in a short period of time.

As these examples demonstrate, your awareness of God's ways of answering prayers will increase if you carefully note any changes that have occurred after praying that could relate to your intention or prayer. Keeping a journal that tracks all of your prayers and the answers you may have received is a great way to do so.

Rather than trying to be perfect in recording such information, I encourage you to emphasize completeness by noting anything that might indicate an answer. Some of what you write may, in fact, be part of an answer. By having sometimes noted more than what is part of God's answer, you will more accurately gain a sense of how God answers you and the ways that you most often notice those answers. Both kinds of awareness will greatly bless you in being better directed by God and drawing closer to Him.

Draw Closer to Our Heavenly Father, the Lord Jesus Christ, and the Holy Spirit by Recording Answers to Your Prayer Requests

As you begin keeping a prayer journal (or improve the one you have), recording the answers that God sends to your prayers will increase your awareness of Him, as well as improve your prayers to better fit with His will. The following questions are designed to assist you to gain more of such benefits:

1. Do you write down the prayer requests you have made?

2. If so, do you note whatever happens after you made such requests?

3. Do you study the possible ways that God might have answered your requests as one means to become more aware of how He answers you?

4. Do you study the possible ways that God might have answered you to become more aware of the ways you are most likely to notice His answers?

5. How does what you observe after praying affect how you pray?

6. How does what you observe affect how close you then feel to God?

7. What would be the best way for you to make such a record of God's answers so it would be useful to you for many years?

8. What could such changes do for your faith?

9. What answers are you now aware of for the first time?

10. Who else might be able to benefit from what you record?

11. How does it make you feel to more seriously treat God's answers to your prayer requests?

Week Four Memory Verse

"Ask, and it will be given to you; seek, and you will find; knock, and it will be opened to you."
(Matthew 7:7, NKJV)

Week Four: Days Five and Six

Consider God's Actions in Answering Your Prayers

But when the multitudes heard it,
they followed Him on foot from the cities.
And when Jesus went out He saw a great multitude; and
He was moved with compassion for them, and healed their sick.
When it was evening, His disciples came to Him, saying,
"This is a deserted place, and the hour is already late.
Send the multitudes away, that they may go
into the villages and buy themselves food."

But Jesus said to them, "They do not need to go away.
You give them something to eat."

And they said to Him,
"We have here only five loaves and two fish."

He said, "Bring them here to Me."

Then He commanded the multitudes to sit down on the grass.
And He took the five loaves and the two fish, and
looking up to heaven, He blessed and broke and gave the loaves
to the disciples; and the disciples gave to the multitudes.

So they all ate and were filled, and they took up twelve baskets
full of the fragments that remained.
Now those who had eaten were about five thousand men,
besides women and children.

— Matthew 14:13-21 (NKJV)

Much as when the disciples in Matthew 14:13-21 (NKJV) expected that Jesus would meet the needs of those present by sending them off to buy food, our prayer requests may generate an answer that is quite different from our expectations. As in this case, God may perceive and act on an opportunity to accomplish more than what we have requested. Praise God when such a wonderful action occurs!

Alternatively, God could, instead, do less than what you prayed for. Such an action is equally worthy of praise. For instance, would doing more cause harm? Or, could it be that God intends to do more in some other way in the future, but hasn't yet acted?

Even if God does exactly what you hoped for when you prayed, wouldn't it be valuable to capture and to describe such an event? At a minimum, your faith would probably be sustained whenever you reviewed this example of His faithfulness.

Notice that there's also a possibility of informing your future prayers. By observing what prayers, done for what purposes and in what ways, elicited various kinds of actions by God, you might well become a more effective communicator to Him.

More significantly, by noticing all the good things that God has done following your prayers, your sense of His closeness, desire to act in response to and with you, and love for you will undoubtedly grow. Consider by comparison that you are probably closest to those family members and friends who have done the most to listen to and help you. If, however, you quickly forgot what such family members and friends had done for you, your closeness to these people could become a thing of the past.

Beyond that, imagine how your children, grandchildren, and others who care about you will respond to seeing the contents of your prayer journal and hearing you relate all that God has done in and through your life. Unless you are very unusual, such individuals (especially those who are not yet believers in and followers of Jesus) know about and appreciate very little of what has occurred in your relationship with God. Consequently, sharing your prayer journal might be an important step toward one of these people coming to faith in or drawing closer to Him. Whenever either result happens, perhaps the result will be an answer to one of your prayers, as well.

Of course, it's not enough to just write down what happened. You should also study the occurrences to gain further understanding of God, His ways, and the relationship you have with Him. As you consider these dimensions of His actions, you will draw closer to Him.

Draw Closer to Our Heavenly Father, the Lord Jesus Christ, and the Holy Spirit by Considering the Actions That Respond to Your Prayers

As you develop your new (or improved) prayer journal, be sure to keep track of and study what actions God takes in response to your prayers. As you do, match the actions to the answers you thought you had received. You may have misunderstood some answers and can now make corrections. Of course, when God fulfills your request in stages, your perception of the original answer may turn out to be partially correct. Adding the perspective of how God acts is wonderful for improving your future prayers, experiencing God more fully by drawing closer to Him, and providing documentation for others to either develop or increase their faith. These questions are designed to assist in such benefits being gained:

1. Do you write down what related actions God takes following your prayer requests?

2. If so, do you later consider what those actions suggest about God, His ways, and the relationship you have with Him?

3. How does considering God's actions that occur after your prayer requests make you feel?

4. As you study the actions God took, do you think about why He might not have taken other actions that were possible responses to your requests?

5. How does what you learned from His actions affect how you pray?

6. How does what you consider about the actions affect how close you then feel to God?

7. What could any increased feeling of closeness to Him do for your faith?

8. What actions are you now aware of for the first time?

9. Who else might benefit from learning about your thoughts concerning His actions?

Week Four Memory Verse

"Ask, and it will be given to you; seek, and you will find; knock, and it will be opened to you."
(Matthew 7:7, NKJV)

Week Five: Days One and Two

Look for God's Hand Working in More Ways

And the power of the Lord was present *to heal them.*
Then behold, men brought on a bed a man who was paralyzed,
whom they sought to bring in and lay before Him.
And when they could not find how they might bring him in,
because of the crowd, they went up on the housetop and
let him down with his *bed through the tiling*
into the midst before Jesus.

When He saw their faith, He said to him,
"Man, your sins are forgiven you."

And the scribes and the Pharisees began to reason, saying,
"Who is this who speaks blasphemies?
Who can forgive sins but God alone?"

But when Jesus perceived their thoughts,
He answered and said to them,
"Why are you reasoning in your hearts? Which is easier, to say,
'Your sins are forgiven you,' or to say, 'Rise up and walk'?
But that you may know that the Son of Man
has power on earth to forgive sins" —
He said to the man who was paralyzed,
"I say to you, arise, take up your bed, and go to your house."

Immediately he rose up before them,
took up what he had been lying on, and
departed to his own house, glorifying God.

— Luke 5:17-25 (NKJV)

Much as happened after His disciples asked Jesus to send the multitudes away to buy food elsewhere, those present when a paralyzed man's friends lowered him down through the roof tiles to reach Jesus were probably surprised by what next occurred. As the dust and grit from disassembling the roof fell into the room, most of the observers might have only expected that Jesus would comment on the intrusion. However, the paralyzed man and his friends were probably seeking healing as one of their prayer requests. Undoubtedly, they were as surprised as the scribes and Pharisees were when, instead, Jesus first forgave the paralyzed man's sins.

By providing such forgiveness, Jesus was clearly indicating that spiritual soundness is more important than being physically whole. When considering the course of eternity, few would argue differently. After all, our physical limitations are gone after this life ends, and we will receive glorified bodies at the resurrection.

After already having surprised everyone, Jesus proceeded to top what He had first done by then healing the paralyzed man, as tangible evidence to the scribes and Pharisees (and any other doubters) that He probably had the power to forgive sins. By doing so, Jesus also showed the others present that His authority was greater than that of the scribes and Pharisees. These people based their exalted social positions on their knowledge of and visible application of the laws of Moses and the traditions of the Jewish people. Undoubtedly, the story presented in these verses spread far and wide, helping to build a firmer foundation for believing in Jesus as being greater than they, as being the Messiah.

There's a simple lesson here for us all: In one event, or series of actions, God may do a great deal more than what first meets the eye as being possible. Naturally, if you had been the paralyzed man, you would probably have concentrated on just receiving your healing. You might later have forgotten what Jesus said about your sins being forgiven. If you were this man's friends, you were probably thrilled about the healing, as well as happy that you didn't have to carry him home. The neutral observers probably remembered the method of arrival and the healing as the foremost events. The scribes and Pharisees probably remembered gnashing their teeth about the so-called blasphemy and having been shown up by Jesus' healing and words. It's only as we step back and consider the whole event from the perspective of not having been there and many years having passed that we can appreciate many more dimensions of what Jesus said and did then.

The recommendation in this lesson for you is straightforward: Whatever God does, take the time to reflect on what all of the related effects might be now and in the future on all those who are and could be affected.

Draw Closer to Our Heavenly Father, the Lord Jesus Christ, and the Holy Spirit by Looking for Their Influence Working in More Ways

God is so much more wise, holy, and powerful than we are that some aspects of His actions and their effects can be almost as though they were invisible to us, simply due to our being overwhelmed by the impact of one part of what He has done. For instance, do you think an ant watching a shoe sole bearing down on it is aware of God sending a bee to cause the person wearing the shoe to change directions before stepping? The following questions are designed to help you notice more of what God does, as well as more of the implications and effects of such actions:

1. When you consider the actions that God takes following your prayer requests, do you seek to find as many effects as possible for yourself and other people?

2. If so, how does what you learn shift how you think about God, His ways, and the relationship you have with Him?

3. How does noticing more of the effects of God's actions following your prayer requests make you feel?

4. How does what you learned from a broader view of His actions affect how you pray?

5. How does what you realize about the full effects of His actions affect how close you then feel to God?

6. What has any increased feeling of closeness with Him done to your faith?

7. Where can you see His hand at work now for the first time?

8. Who else might benefit from learning about your observations concerning the full effects of His actions?

9. How can you be sure to look for more effects of God's future actions?

Week Five Memory Verse

"Well *done*, good and faithful servant; you were faithful over a few things, I will make you ruler over many things. Enter into the joy of your lord." (Matthew 25:21, NKJV)

Week Five: Days Three and Four

Receive More Instructions from God

"*For* the kingdom of heaven is *like a man traveling to a far country,*
who called his own servants and delivered his goods to them.
And to one he gave five talents, to another two, and to another one,
to each according to his own ability; and immediately he went on a journey.

"*Then he who had received the five talents went and traded with them,*
and made another five talents. And likewise he who had received *two*
gained two more also. But he who had received one went and dug in the ground,
and hid his lord's money. After a long time the lord of those servants
came and settled accounts with them.

"*So he who had received five talents came and brought five other talents, saying,*
'Lord, you delivered to me five talents;
look, I have gained five more talents besides them.'

"*His lord said to him, 'Well* done, *good and faithful servant;*
you were faithful over a few things, I will make you ruler
over many things. Enter into the joy of your lord.'

"*He also who had received two talents came and said,*
'Lord, you delivered to me two talents;
look, I have gained two more talents besides them.'

"*His lord said to him, 'Well* done, *good and faithful servant;*
you have been faithful over a few things, I will make you ruler
over many things. Enter into the joy of your lord.'

"*Then he who had received the one talent came and said, 'Lord, I knew you*
to be a hard man, reaping where you have not sown, and gathering where you
have not scattered seed. And I was afraid, and went and hid your talent
in the ground. Look, there *you have* what is *yours.'*

"But his lord answered and said to him,
'You wicked and lazy servant, you knew that I reap where I have not sown,
and gather where I have not scattered seed. So you ought to have deposited
my money with the bankers, and at my coming I would have received back
my own with interest. Therefore take the talent from him,
and give it to him who has ten talents.

"For to everyone who has, more will be given, and he will have abundance;
but from him who does not have, even what he has will be taken away.'"

— Matthew 25:14-29 (NKJV)

Much as the paralyzed man and those present then experienced, all the servants in this parable (had they been actual people, rather than fictional characters) would probably have been surprised by their lord's reactions. Surely, the first two of such servants would have expected to receive little, if anything, for having acted rightly and been successful. Being told that they would become rulers over many things would have been quite a nice surprise, perhaps even one that could have been a little daunting to all but the most confident servants. Of course, the servant who "protected" the talent probably thought there would be no consequences. This last servant misread his lord, failing to appreciate that a reasonable attempt to increase the talent had been expected. This servant was not only scolded; he also lost sovereignty over the resource that had been entrusted to him.

Rather than spend more time conjecturing about the potential reactions of the parable's fictional servants, let's look at some implications of the Parable of the Talents for us. First, we should, of course, view the "lord" in this case as being God. Second, the servants are believers, and we stand in their shoes with relation to God. Third, God is providing resources commensurate with the abilities each believer has. While God provides us each with natural talents (rather than just financial resources), it is only through the proper exercise of such talents that their potential is turned into our actual abilities. Consequently, the parable suggests that God will give us bigger responsibilities and the resources to accomplish them well after we are faithful in developing our personal abilities. The uneven provision of added resources to accomplish still more will be commensurate to such abilities. Fourth, after we add to and successfully apply our abilities for God's Kingdom, we will receive greater responsibilities and resources. Rewarding successful application of abilities is made explicit in the parable by those who increased the talents (the first two servants) being told they would rule over many things. Just in case that point had escaped us, the third servant's talent is taken away and entrusted to the first servant, so that he now has charge of eleven talents. Fifth, and most uncomfortably for some readers who have not been using their talents and abilities to serve God, the third servant lost all the resources and authority that God had initially given him.

The point for us in this lesson is a simple, but profound, one: After being faithful in applying the talents, abilities, and resources that God has given us for His purposes, He will increase what He asks us to do while providing whatever is needed to succeed. We should always be seeking to gain such a vote of confidence from Him, and listening and looking for His instructions for working on our next assignment. If we miss these instructions, we will end up being like the third servant, someone who hasn't been faithful to Him and who will be punished by losing resources needed to accomplish His will. I'm sure you don't want that to happen.

This point can be hard to act on because the increase in responsibilities may be quite daunting. In the parable, the servants were initially taking care of valuable objects. A talent of silver then weighed a little less than 100 pounds, and a talent of gold was twice that weight. In today's terms, either one would be worth a significant sum. At around $20 an ounce for silver, a talent of it would be worth over $30,000. At around $1,000 for an ounce of gold, a talent of this precious metal would be worth over $3 million. Yet, graduating from trading or investing substantial sums of money to actually ruling (which implies authority and power over people) for God could leave many believers with at least some queasiness in their stomachs.

Unlike the third servant, we should not let fear guide us. God will give us what we need to succeed, and He will be with us as we do our work … unlike the absent lord in the parable. If what we can do in our own strength isn't enough, He will provide what's needed. Keep listening and watching, and be prepared to act!

Draw Closer to Our Heavenly Father, the Lord Jesus Christ, and the Holy Spirit by Listening and Looking for More Instructions

As humans, we can easily become tired, discouraged, disoriented, and even a bit lost. God wants to help us whenever one of those circumstances occurs. Yet, His instructions can temporarily increase the weight we feel for addressing our responsibilities, especially when our faith is inadequate at that moment to simply rely on Him to get us where we should be. After succeeding in what He has asked, sensing His presence through new instructions can be even more helpful than seeing a light at the end of a tunnel for drawing us next in the right direction and towards the best path. The following questions are designed to help you do so:

1. When you have just accomplished a task for God, do you expect that you will receive new instructions entailing bigger responsibilities and challenges?

2. When you receive new instructions, how do they shift how you think about God, His ways, and the relationship you have with Him?

3. How does noticing God's new instructions make you feel?

4. How do the new instructions affect how you pray?

5. How does receiving the new directions affect how close you then feel to God?

6. What has any increased feeling of closeness with Him done to your faith?

7. What lessons have you drawn from having received new instructions from God?

8. How have those lessons differed when the new instructions called for you taking on bigger challenges and responsibilities for God's Kingdom than felt comfortable to you?

9. What new instructions from Him do you now perceive?

10. Who else might benefit from learning about your experiences with receiving new instructions from God?

Week Five Memory Verse

"Well *done*, good and faithful servant; you were faithful over a few things, I will make you ruler over many things. Enter into the joy of your lord." (Matthew 25:21, NKJV)

Week Five: Days Five and Six

Praise God with More Joy

So it was, when the angels had gone away from them into heaven,
that the shepherds said to one another,
"Let us now go to Bethlehem and
see this thing that has come to pass,
which the Lord has made known to us."

And they came with haste and found Mary and Joseph,
and the Babe lying in a manger.

Now when they had seen Him, *they made widely known*
the saying which was told them concerning this Child.
And all those who heard it marveled at those things
which were told them by the shepherds.

But Mary kept all these things and pondered them *in her heart.*

Then the shepherds returned,
glorifying and praising God
for all the things that they had heard and seen,
as it was told them.

— Luke 2:15-20 (NKJV)

On the night Jesus was born, some shepherds in the fields were told by an angel of the wonderful event and how to recognize their Savior. Although they were not specifically directed to seek Him, they wisely chose to draw closer to God by doing so. Their reaction to these events was to tell many people about the visitation from the angel and seeing Jesus. After fulfilling the opportunity God had sent them, the shepherds returned to the fields, glorifying and praising God for what they had seen and heard.

Similarly, our desire to praise God with more joy will increase after we have drawn closer to Him through following His instructions and engaging in the opportunities for drawing closer that He sends.

Consider the alternative. What if you do not follow His instructions and seek opportunities to draw closer? Well, your relationship with Him is going to suffer … and you are going to miss some amazing experiences. Just think what it would have been like to have been a shepherd on that glorious night who decided to stay with the sheep, rather than seek Jesus. The decision would have probably felt all right initially … at least until the other shepherds returned and related all that had occurred with Joseph, Mary, and the baby Jesus. If you don't follow His directions, you might be missing out on something equally amazing that God has intended since before the creation for you to enjoy. Don't let that happen.

Imagine, instead, being treated to ever greater and more wonderful opportunities to draw closer to God. Just think of how much joy you would feel as you glorified and praised Him after such experiences!

Draw Closer to Our Heavenly Father, the Lord Jesus Christ, and the Holy Spirit by Praising Them with More Joy

In the middle of running a marathon (following a typically up-and-down course over more than 26 miles), the only temporary relief such a runner might receive is from hearing someone cheer. The person who provides that encouragement, in turn, receives a benefit if the runner then smiles and strides with more enthusiasm and energy. For each of us, accomplishing God's plans can feel like being in the middle of such a long and challenging race. Being able to refocus our attention on appreciating what He has provided can help us feel His encouragement by being filled with His joy. The following questions can help you to feel more joy as you partner with Him to advance His Kingdom:

1. When you accomplish a task for God, do you expect that you will be filled with more joy and praise Him more enthusiastically?

2. When you receive new instructions from God, how do they change the joy you feel when thinking about Him, His ways, and the relationship you have with Him?

3. How does the increased joy you feel affect how you pray?

4. How does the increased joy you feel affect how you praise Him?

5. What has the increased feeling of joy from being with and obeying Him done to your faith?

6. What lessons have you drawn about receiving such joy from God?

7. How has the increased joy affected how you feel when God's new instructions have called for you to take on bigger challenges and responsibilities for His Kingdom?

8. What can you do now and in the future to feel more of God's joy when you praise Him?

9. Who else might benefit from learning about your experiences with receiving more joy from God?

Week Five Memory Verse

"Well *done*, good and faithful servant; you were faithful over a few things, I will make you ruler over many things. Enter into the joy of your lord." (Matthew 25:21, NKJV)

Part Four:

Help Expand and Improve God's Kingdom

"Assuredly, I say to you, there is no one
who has left house or parents or brothers or wife or children,
for the sake of the kingdom of God,
who shall not receive many times more in this present time,
and in the age to come eternal life."

— Luke 18:29-30 (NKJV)

We now begin the final part of *Disciple*. I thank you for your kind attention to the first 45 lessons. I pray that these activities have blessed you in wonderful ways.

By now experiencing God more fully, living the Gospel, and drawing closer to our Heavenly Father, the Lord Jesus Christ, and the Holy Spirit, you have become more aware of and effective in playing the role planned by God for you to help expand and improve His Kingdom. Keeping those valuable lessons in mind, we now shift to helping you become even more fruitful in your work for the Kingdom.

We start by considering the gifts and talents God has given you. From that topic, we will move on to some practical steps for keeping your actions better aligned with God's intentions. The lessons culminate with helping others gain the experiences you have had through reading and applying *Disciple*.

May God abundantly bless and support you while engaging in new experiences during these next 15 lessons.

Week One: Days One and Two

Consider How Your Gifts and Talents Can Better Serve God

As each one has received a gift,
minister it to one another,
as good stewards of the manifold grace of God.

— 1 Peter 4:10 (NKJV)

There are diversities of gifts, but the same Spirit.
There are differences of ministries, but the same Lord.
And there are diversities of activities,
but it is the same God who works all in all.
But the manifestation of the Spirit is
given to each one for the profit of all:

For as the body is one and has many members,
but all the members of that one body, being many,
are one body, so also is Christ.
For by one Spirit we were all baptized into one body —
Jews or Greeks, whether slaves or free —
and have all been made to drink into one Spirit.

— 1 Corinthians 12:4-7, 12-13 (NKJV)

Let's begin by defining "gifts" and "talents." By gifts, I mean spiritual gifts, those that are brought by the Holy Spirit to all believers. As 1 Corinthians 12:4 (NKJV) tells us, there are diversities of such gifts. God chooses gifts to give each believer that will be useful for the activities that He has planned for each person to do in serving His Kingdom. Notice that 1 Peter 4:10 (NKJV) tells us that such gifts should be used for ministering God's grace to one another. If we each do our part, then the diversity of these gifts combines to make the whole body of believers more effective for His purposes.

Talents are also God-given, but these are given to everyone, believer and nonbeliever alike. We can use talents to develop personal abilities through diligent application. Thus, someone might have so-called perfect pitch that enables him or her to know what note is being played. However, that talent won't be of much value for composing sacred music unless the person with the talent develops ability in making such an application.

Gifts and talents are two of the ways that God makes us unique. Since He designed us in a certain way in terms of these gifts and talents, we can learn more about His intentions and plans for us by considering what those gifts and talents are, as well as how they might be applied to expand and improve His Kingdom.

Many people are unsure of what their spiritual gifts are. A number of online questionnaires and tests can be used to gain some ideas of what those gifts might be. If you search online for subjects such as "spiritual gifts questionnaire" or "spiritual gifts test," you should be able to find several resources that could be helpful to you. You may learn even more by employing more than one such resource. For instance, my list of spiritual gifts turns out a bit differently depending on which questionnaires and tests I use. Perhaps your list will, too. After using such resources, I suggest you ask believers who know you well to comment on their sense of your possible gifts. Finally, ask God to guide you in identifying the correct ones.

In terms of your talents, you probably have a better idea. Through observing others during family, school, and personal activities, you could have developed a good sense of what is easier for you to do well than for most other people. As you consider those areas, also think about where you have done the most to develop any talents into abilities. Again, you can ask others to share their perceptions. Of course, prayer is also a great way to help identify or validate your talents.

When you have a pretty good idea of what your gifts and talents are, I suggest you meet with a pastor or lay leader at your church who knows about the various ways that believers have been fruitful for God's Kingdom to discuss how your gifts and talents might be applied. I make that suggestion because my students in past discipleship classes often reported having no idea of who would benefit or how from what they could provide.

If you would like to conduct some research before such a discussion, contact organizations that work to advance God's Kingdom and appear to be looking for either employees or volunteers. Share what you have learned about yourself and ask for suggestions about how you might be of assistance to each organization.

Take whatever information you obtain and pray for God's guidance about serving these or other needs. Be especially open to acting on His answers to your prayers in this regard. Keep in mind that although He may have something grand planned for you at some future point in your life, in the beginning your experiences with using gifts and talents will often be quite humble ones. Eagerly engage in what He calls you to do. There may be unexpectedly rewarding and fruitful ways to serve His Kingdom in even the most humble roles that you are uniquely equipped to accomplish.

Help Expand and Improve God's Kingdom by Considering How Your Gifts and Talents Can Better Serve Him

You may already be using some of your spiritual gifts and personal talents to expand and improve God's Kingdom. It's good to consider how you could accomplish even more in applying those gifts and talents, as well as how to begin using other ones that you either didn't realize you had or that you haven't been applying for His purposes. The following questions are designed to help you begin to do so through experiencing what it means to better understand God's intentions for you through the gifts and talents He has provided:

1. What spiritual gifts do you think you have now before making any further investigations?

2. What other spiritual gifts did you uncover through your investigations related to this lesson?

3. What talents do you think you have before any further investigating?

4. What other talents did you uncover through your investigations related to this lesson?

5. How does considering all those gifts and talents affect your desire to experience and know God more fully?

6. How are you applying all those gifts and talents now to expand and improve His Kingdom?

7. How else do you feel called to do so?

8. How does it make you feel to not be using some of your gifts and talents to their full potential for the Kingdom?

9. What do you want to say to Him now about what you will begin doing today?

10. How did you feel after saying so?

11. What lessons can you share with other believers based on applying this lesson?

12. How will you remain more aware of your gifts and talents and their fruitfulness for God's Kingdom in the future?

<u>Week One Memory Verse</u>

"A good man out of the good treasure of his heart brings forth good things, and an evil man out of the evil treasure brings forth evil things." (Matthew 12:35, NKJV)

Week One: Days Three and Four

Experience How Serving God Most Energizes You

"Go into the village opposite you,
where as you enter you will find a colt tied,
on which no one has ever sat. Loose it and bring it here."

Then they brought him to Jesus.
And they threw their own clothes on the colt,
and they set Jesus on him. And as He went,
many spread their clothes on the road.

Then, as He was now drawing near
the descent of the Mount of Olives,
the whole multitude of the disciples began to
rejoice and praise God with a loud voice
for all the mighty works they had seen, saying:

"'Blessed is the King who comes in the name of the LORD!'
Peace in heaven and glory in the highest!"

— Luke 19:30, 35-38 (NKJV)

Now it came to pass, while He blessed them,
that He was parted from them and
carried up into heaven.
And they worshiped Him, and
returned to Jerusalem with great joy,
and were continually in the temple
praising and blessing God. Amen.

— Luke 24:51-53 (NKJV)

The verses above describe two occasions when the Bible tells us that believers in Jesus experienced great joy: The first occasion was on Palm Sunday when Jesus triumphantly entered Jerusalem, and the second occurred on the day of Ascension, just after that blessed event. While it's easy to imagine that each person present experienced the same amount of joy, there could have been variations in the joy that was felt ... simply due to differences in how each person had been created by God to experience that wonderful emotion. However, for those who experienced the most joy, this feeling undoubtedly was a source of energy for desiring to be more fruitful and supporting His will, including by simply praising and blessing Him.

141

While anticipation of serving God's will may or may not provide joy (consider Jesus in the garden of Gethsemane prior to His betrayal), part of the reward for serving faithfully will often be to experience more joy after so doing. We also know from the Parable of the Talents that God will provide more resources to those who make good use of the ones that He has previously provided. Through the Holy Spirit, we also receive power from God, power that both energizes us and also permits more to be accomplished by our efforts.

Thus, by considering the experiences we have had with being energized by serving God, we can gain insights into what He has prepared for and called us to do. If we then experiment by serving Him in new ways, especially in those suggested by our gifts and talents He has provided, we can also find other ways that serving Him will energize us.

Receiving such increased energy while or after serving God is a certain sign of His approval and support for our activities. Even more accurately than a compass usually points us towards magnetic north, increased energy during or after Godly service will tell us that we have done the right thing.

Help Expand and Improve God's Kingdom by Experiencing How Serving God Most Energizes You

You may already be gaining enormous energy from certain ways that you help improve and expand God's Kingdom. It's good to consider how you could accomplish even more by gaining still more energy, as well as receiving such energy infusions more often. You should draw on your experiences when such energizing has occurred, as well as when it has not, to direct your activities for God. In addition, as you apply your gifts and talents in new ways, notice which applications create increased energy in you. The following questions are designed to help you assess past and new experiences to gain this understanding:

1. When has serving God given you a substantial increase in energy?

2. Do such energy increases often occur when you serve in these ways?

3. When has serving God not increased your energy?

4. Does such a lack of increased energy usually occur when you serve in these ways?

5. How does either receiving or not receiving increased energy from serving God affect your faith?

6. Are there gifts and talents that you have not yet used to expand and improve God's Kingdom?

7. If so, how did your first experiences with applying such gifts and talents in Godly service (beginning today) affect your energy?

8. How does it feel to discover new ways to serve God that increase the energy you receive from Him?

9. As a result, what do you want to say to Him now about what you will do?

10. How did you feel after saying so?

11. What lessons can you share with other believers based on applying this lesson?

12. How will you uncover new ways of gaining increased energy in service to Him?

Week One Memory Verse

"A good man out of the good treasure of his heart brings forth good things, and an evil man out of the evil treasure brings forth evil things." (Matthew 12:35, NKJV)

Week One: Days Five and Six

Feel How Serving God Touches Your Heart

"A good man out of the good treasure of his heart
brings forth good things, and
an evil man out of the evil treasure
brings forth evil things."

— Matthew 12:35 (NKJV)

Matthew 12:35 (NKJV) reminds us that the heart is the source of making ethical decisions and taking actions. When your heart is filled with God's goodness, you will want to express that goodness in ways that will serve Him and enhance life for everyone. When your heart, instead, is partially or completely compromised by the evil one, evil desires will lead to evil deeds.

For the purposes of this lesson, your heart connection to God should be considered from two perspectives: before and after you do something intended to expand and improve His Kingdom. The heart appeal of something that you have done before is based, of course, in part on your prior experience with performing this kind of service for the Kingdom. However, for something you haven't done before, the heart appeal will mostly be coming from how God constructed you and prepared your life to notice and be more sensitive to certain people, things, and situations. Keep in mind that you need to be sure you have enough information for your heart to be touched in the way God intended. For instance, if an organization that serves others doesn't provide much information about what it does, your heart might not be touched. If, instead, you discover that many people are helped in a way that God intended for you to perform, the heart appeal should be quite strong. So keep exposing yourself to new, good activities so that your heart can help lead you to the right actions for serving Him.

After having served in a way that your heart had called you to do, consider whether that heart appeal is stronger, the same, or weaker. If the experience leaves you feeling more strongly attracted to repeating the service, you are probably on the right track. Feeling about the same can also be an indication to continue. However, if your heart appeal is reduced, you may not yet be serving in the best way. Could it be that a different role or task would be closer to your calling from God? Might a different organization offer an activity that provides more heart appeal for you?

Finally, if some form of service seems to attract your attention to doing sinful things, you've got a problem you need to immediately address. Take that problem to God in prayer, and pay close attention to His answer. Also, investigate if there are other ways to serve that don't cause such harmful distractions for you.

Help Expand and Improve God's Kingdom by Feeling How Serving God Touches Your Heart

You are surely doing at least some things for improving and expanding God's Kingdom that have touched and continue to touch your heart. It's good to investigate if there are other ways to serve that will touch your heart as much or more. In such seeking, especially look into opportunities to apply more of your gifts and talents, as well as the same ones you have been applying in new, more heartfelt ways. As you have new experiences in serving, pay close attention to how your heart is affected before, during, and after each experience. The following questions will help you assess new experiences to gain such understanding:

1. When has serving God increased your heartfelt desire to do more of the same?

2. Do such increases in heartfelt desires to do more of the same often occur when you serve in these ways?

3. When has serving God *not* increased your heartfelt desire to do more?

4. Does such a lack of increased desire usually occur when you serve in these ways?

5. How does either receiving or not receiving increased desire from serving God affect your faith?

6. Are there gifts and talents that you have not yet used to expand and improve God's Kingdom?

7. If so, how did your first experiences with applying those gifts and talents in Godly service (beginning today) affect your heart's desire to do more?

8. How does it feel to discover new ways to serve God that increase your desire to serve Him and feel rewarded by the service?

9. As a result, what do you want to say to Him now about what you will do?

10. How did you feel after saying so?

11. What lessons can you share with other believers based on applying this lesson?

12. How will you increase your future experiences of new ways to serve Him?

Week One Memory Verse

"A good man out of the good treasure of his heart brings forth good things, and an evil man out of the evil treasure brings forth evil things." (Matthew 12:35, NKJV)

Week Two: Days One and Two

Write Your Testimony

But the angel answered and said to the women,
"Do not be afraid, for I know that you seek Jesus who was crucified.
He is not here; for He is risen, as He said.
Come, see the place where the Lord lay.
And go quickly and tell His disciples that He is risen from the dead,
and indeed He is going before you into Galilee;
there you will see Him. Behold, I have told you."

So they went out quickly from the tomb
with fear and great joy, and ran to bring His disciples word.

And as they went to tell His disciples, behold,
Jesus met them, saying, "Rejoice!"
So they came and held Him by the feet and worshiped Him.

Then Jesus said to them, "Do not be afraid.
Go and tell My brethren to go to Galilee,
and there they will see Me."

— Matthew 28:5-10 (NKJV)

Matthew 28:5-10 (NKJV) reminds us that if no one who observed that Jesus had risen from the dead had ever shared that information, you and I might not be believers today. In less dramatic fashion, God has given you experiences with Him that will move others to want to draw nearer to Him, whether they are currently believers or merely curious. Just before He ascended into Heaven, Jesus told His disciples to take the Gospel to all nations (one version of the Great Commission is found in Matthew 28:18-20, NKJV). Writing and sharing your testimony are two ways to help accomplish that wonderful assignment from Him.

Here are a few of my favorite reasons for writing and sharing your testimony:

• Someone might seek Salvation.
• The writing and sharing will help bring you closer to God.
• The information will strengthen believers and help to renew their faith.
• Learning about your experiences will bring added hope that God will help with problems.
• Your life will demonstrate a way of being with God that others will want to seek.

There are many good sources of instructions for writing a testimony. Feel free to investigate several of them. As you prepare your testimony, let the Holy Spirit guide you in determining what to share and how to provide the information. Keep what you share brief and meaningful.

Even if you feel that you have no writing skill, someone in your church probably does and can help you revise your story so it will be more understandable. If such a person isn't in your church, many inexpensive editors can be found by searching online.

As part of a global contest to find better ways to witness, I was honored by God with an opportunity to describe some good ways to write and share testimonies. Chapter 5 in *Witnessing Made Easy: Yes, You Can Make a Difference* (Jubilee Worship Center Step by Step Press, 2010) provides instructions that might be helpful for stimulating your thinking and writing.

In a standalone testimony designed to be read by people who are not believers, consider the benefits of including the following sections, as paraphrased here from a list on page 83 of the above book:

1. God exists.
2. God can do what people cannot do.
3. God changed my life by saving my soul.
4. God gave me joy while sharing my faith.
5. God wants to give you blessings when you receive Salvation.
6. God presents Salvation as a gift when you follow Him.
7. God will improve your life as a new Christian when you follow His directions.
8. You can get more information about Salvation from me, another witness, and my church.

If you would like an example of a testimony that includes all these elements or have questions about what to write, please feel free to contact Jim Barbarossa, one of the coauthors of *Witnessing Made Easy*, who can be contacted at Jim@step-by-step.org/.

Help Expand and Improve God's Kingdom by Writing Your Testimony

You have probably told some people how you came to faith and what knowing Jesus as your Lord and Savior has meant to you. If you recall the questions and reactions you received to such sharing, these can help guide what to include in your testimony. Also, ask the Holy Spirit to direct you in what to share. As you prepare to write, realize that you don't have to provide embarrassing details unless called by God to do so. The following questions will help you decide what to include:

1. How do you know that God exists?

2. What can God do that people cannot?

3. How have you experienced His amazing power?

4. What was your life like before you were saved?

5. How has Salvation improved your life?

6. What joyful experiences have you had in sharing your faith?

7. What blessings have you received from gaining Salvation?

8. What blessings should others expect to receive from Salvation?

9. Can you describe how to confess sins, repent, and accept Jesus as Lord and Savior?

10. If not, will you take the time to learn how to do so now?

11. What should a new believer do next after accepting Salvation?

12. If you don't know, will you take the time to learn the answer now?

13. Who else can answer the questions raised by someone who reads your testimony?

Week Two Memory Verse

"Follow Me, and I will make you fishers of men." (Matthew 4:19, NKJV)

Week Two: Days Three and Four

Share Your Testimony

Later He appeared to the eleven as they sat at the table; and
He rebuked their unbelief and hardness of heart,
because they did not believe those
who had seen Him after He had risen.

And He said to them,
"Go into all the world and preach the gospel to every creature.
He who believes and is baptized will be saved; but
he who does not believe will be condemned."

— Mark 16:14-16 (NKJV)

Mark 16:14-16 (NKJV) mentions two important elements about belief and sharing the Gospel not found in the most often quoted version of Jesus' Great Commission (Matthew 28:19-20, NKJV): the importance of believing those who have had direct experiences with God and of sharing the Gospel with "every creature." Obviously, effective communications are more the responsibility of the speaker or writer than they are of the hearer or reader, but Jesus is making it clear that people who know Him well (such as the eleven loyal disciples) should believe the testimonies of others. The second element reminds us that all Creation is fallen, including the animals, and needs to be restored and maintained by human efforts until Jesus returns. You might remember that St. Francis was credited with treating birds and other animals as his brothers and sisters, and preaching to them.

Naturally, if those who know Jesus best should become more believing after they hear testimonies, how much more does it make sense that those who know Him best also share their own testimonies with those who don't yet know Him? Yet many people with wonderful testimonies that affirm the Gospel don't share them.

Why? Many polls have been conducted on the subject of what causes such silence. I won't cite a particular one, but common reasons reported for not sharing the Gospel include:

- Feeling inadequate to answer questions that a reader or hearer might have
- Being afraid of offending someone who reads or hears
- Having concerns about getting into a dispute
- Feeling shy about speaking to other people about anything personal

After having shared my testimony with large numbers of people over a great many years, it's my opinion that such reasons need not concern anyone and that the actual source for such views is usually the devil whispering his lies into our minds. Try reading Scripture as you prepare to share your testimony, and I think you'll come to feel pretty comfortable as you hand someone your testimony and speak about it. I especially recommend Ephesians 6:10-18 (NKJV) for the purpose of helping you feel good about and while testifying. These verses are quoted here:

Finally, my brethren, be strong in the Lord and in the power of His might. Put on the whole armor of God, that you may be able to stand against the wiles of the devil. For we do not wrestle against flesh and blood, but against principalities, against powers, against the rulers of the darkness of this age, against spiritual *hosts* of wickedness in the heavenly *places*. Therefore take up the whole armor of God, that you may be able to withstand in the evil day, and having done all, to stand.

Stand therefore, having girded your waist with truth, having put on the breastplate of righteousness, and having shod your feet with the preparation of the gospel of peace; above all, taking the shield of faith with which you will be able to quench all the fiery darts of the wicked one. And take the helmet of salvation, and the sword of the Spirit, which is the word of God; praying always with all prayer and supplication in the Spirit, being watchful to this end with all perseverance and supplication for all the saints — ....

Let me describe my experiences in sharing my testimony. First, I have never been asked a question about my testimony that a 10-year-old with limited knowledge could not have easily and comfortably answered. Sharing my testimony has certainly not led to anything resembling a theological debate. Second, I have never had someone act as if or say that she or he was offended or upset by hearing or reading my testimony. Third, I have never heard a cross word or had a disagreement about my testimony. Fourth, those who have read or heard my testimony have usually been fascinated by what they learned. In person, questions have always been asked that indicated the person wanted to know more. In addition, I have always been able to develop a closer relationship with someone I know by sharing my testimony.

Of course, you don't yet have as much experience as I do. If you get your feet wet slowly, it can feel comfortable finding out what it's like to share your testimony. An advantage of having a written testimony is that you can simply hand or send it to someone. Doing either one is much less intimidating than attempting to describe your testimony in person for the first time. As you first share your written testimony with someone, I suggest you do so with a more experienced sharer who can both demonstrate what to do and encourage you. After doing so feels comfortable, continue to share your testimony with nonbelievers while with an experienced sharer. After ten or so experiences, you'll probably feel comfortable handing someone your testimony when an appropriate moment arises to do so.

Think about the times when such opportunities have arisen. As you do, realize that you can plant seeds to help such opportunities develop by asking others questions to learn more about them. For instance, asking questions such as "What do you do on Sundays?", "Do you attend church?", or "Do you believe in God?" can lead to a discussion of personal beliefs. After listening attentively and asking the other person questions, it's natural at some point to provide a written testimony that explains your experiences. You can precede such an offering with a query about whether the other person would like to know how you came to faith and what having faith has been like.

After you become comfortable with sharing your written testimony, you'll eventually reach the point where you can paraphrase relevant portions of it to include in a discussion about faith and life. When you feel ready to do so, I suggest you have someone who is experienced in talking about his or her faith demonstrate such a conversation with a nonbeliever and encourage you to join in doing the same. After a handful of such supported experiences, you'll gain comfort in speaking to nonbelievers, rather than only handing out your written testimony. Of course, you can do both in the course of one discussion.

As you speak, keep in mind that only the Holy Spirit can lead someone to accept Salvation. If someone doesn't immediately act based on receiving your testimony, realize you have still planted a seed that can grow into Salvation. I have never personally had the experience of sharing my testimony and having someone immediately accept Jesus. Many people will contribute along the way to most people becoming saved. Just be sure to do the part that God calls for you to play. These words of the Apostle Paul provide a helpful perspective:

Who then is Paul, and who *is* Apollos, but ministers through whom you believed, as the Lord gave to each one? I planted, Apollos watered, but God gave the increase. So then neither he who plants is anything, nor he who waters, but God who gives the increase. Now he who plants and he who waters are one, and each one will receive his own reward according to his own labor. (1 Corinthians 3:5-8, NKJV)

Help Expand and Improve God's Kingdom by Sharing Your Testimony

You have probably been praying that certain people (such as family members, friends, neighbors, co-workers, and those you often see) would accept Jesus as Lord and Savior. Now that you have written your testimony, you'll find that sharing your experiences with God can be a part of helping such nonbelievers to assess the Salvation opportunity. Also, pray daily for the Holy Spirit to open a door for you to share. Then, follow His lead in what and how to share. These questions will help you prepare to do so more effectively and comfortably:

1. In what situations would you feel comfortable sharing your written testimony?

2. Who has experience in doing so and could go with you as you do?

3. In what other ways would you like to eventually share your written testimony?

4. Who could provide ideas for how to do so?

5. Who could help you practice these new methods?

6. Under what circumstances would you feel comfortable briefly describing your testimony?

7. What questions would you feel comfortable asking someone that might lead to knowing her or him better and possibly having a conversation in which you would comfortably and naturally share your experiences with God?

8. Who could go with you and participate in such conversations until you felt comfortable doing so on your own?

9. What signs from the Holy Spirit would you look for in determining how to share your testimony with a specific person?

10. How can you share your testimony in ways that demonstrate Christ's love for you?

11. What can you do today to take the first step towards sharing your testimony in a new way?

12. How did you feel as you took that step?

13. What lessons would you share with others about your experience in doing so?

14. How can you continue to grow in effectively serving God's Kingdom through sharing your testimony?

Week Two Memory Verse

"Follow Me, and I will make you fishers of men." (Matthew 4:19, NKJV)

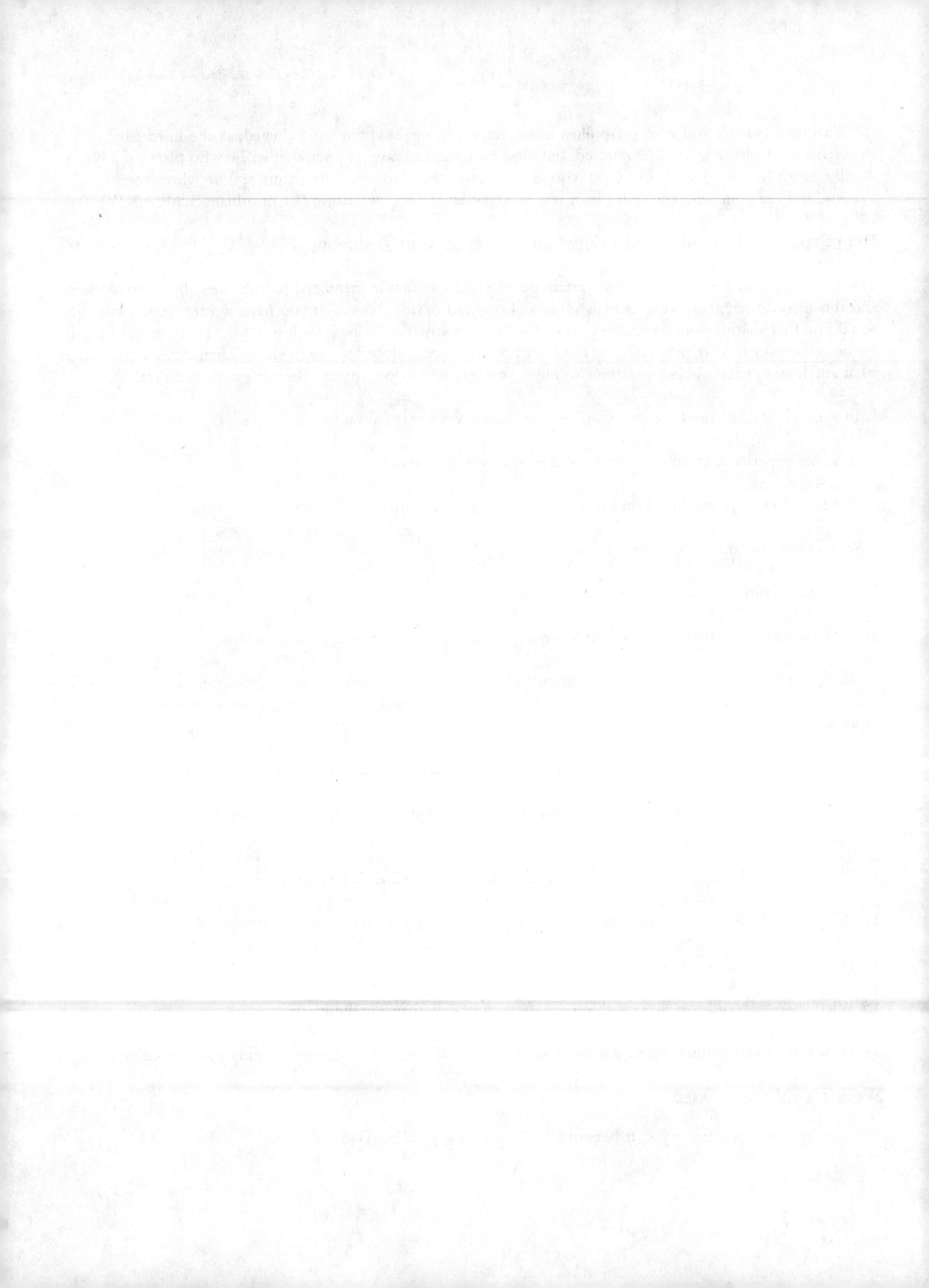

Week Two: Days Five and Six

Make Your Testimony Accessible

Then He said to them,
"Follow Me, and I will make you fishers of men."

— Matthew 4:19 (NKJV)

Matthew 4:19 (NKJV) contains one of the most often quoted statements made by Jesus. In this verse, He was speaking to Simon (later renamed as Peter by Jesus) and Andrew, Simon's brother, who were fishermen. If we connect this statement to the sharing the Gospel aspect of the Great Commission, we can see that Jesus has a potential role for all saved people to play in helping nonbelievers gain Salvation and lead fruitful lives in God's Kingdom.

While the prior two lessons focused on personally sharing a testimony in print or through conversation, such direct involvements are only two ways that your testimony can play a role in serving God's Kingdom. You can also make your testimony accessible for others to discover and interact with on their own.

Let me explain. The Christian books I've written, for instance, include some version of my testimony (including the one in Appendix B). While you may not be a professional writer, you can make written references to your faith available to others. By doing so, you will probably make some people curious to know more about your faith and what it has meant to you.

One opportunity for doing so that I've taken advantage of is by sharing my testimony in books of testimonies that are distributed by eager witnesses. While I recommend that every church provide such an opportunity for its believers, most churches do not. If you would like to explore sharing your testimony in this way, contact Jim Barbarossa at jim@step-by-step.org/. He and his wife, Carla, have provided me with such opportunities, and they can probably accommodate you, as well. There is often a cost involved to cover printing and shipping expenses for providing you with an appropriate number of books to share. Other witnesses will do the same, and your testimony will eventually be read by many thousands of people. Jim and Carla can even help find someone to help you write your testimony.

A less expensive alternative is to simply include all or portions of your testimony on social media sites where the information would be relevant and of interest to those you connect with there. If it makes sense to only direct someone to your testimony, a link can simply be added to almost any such site to take someone to a blog page containing your testimony. Blogs can be started and maintained for free using excellent resources at sites such as www.blogger.com/.

Audio files can also be easily created and linked to your social media pages. If you want to share ongoing observations about your experiences with God, you could do so by creating a podcast subscription that hearers can listen to.

Of course, many people prefer to view a brief video. If your computer or smartphone has a camera, you can record your testimony and place it on a site such as www.youtube.com/. By providing links to such a video testimony on your social media pages, you can also attract those who don't know you well but are curious to learn more. Some of those who are interested in what you say may tell others to view or hear your testimony.

I'm sure you'll think of better ideas than those I have just shared, and I would be delighted to learn about them. I will include such ideas in future editions of *Disciple* with credit to you. To let me know your ideas, just contact me at donmitchell@fastforward400.com/.

Help Expand and Improve God's Kingdom by Making Your Testimony Accessible

While it would be a great joy to be present when the Holy Spirit moves someone's heart to seek information about gaining Salvation and becoming fruitful for God's Kingdom, being present may not be likely. However, if your testimony is accessible enough, you can be indirectly present through it at such a moment. While accessing your testimony may not be as effective as speaking with you face to face, reading, hearing, or seeing the testimony can provide an incentive to seek you out to learn more when you are available. The following questions will help you to extend the reach of your testimony by increasing its accessibility:

1. In what ways could a written version of your testimony become available at more times and to which people when you are not present?

2. Which of those ways does the Holy Spirit direct you to implement?

3. In what ways could an audio version of your testimony and experiences with God be made available?

4. Which of those ways does the Holy Spirit direct you to do?

5. How could video versions of your testimony and experiences with God be made available?

6. Which of those ways does the Holy Spirit direct you to provide?

7. Who could help you learn about and employ such methods?

8. What can you do today to take a step towards making your testimony more accessible?

9. How did you feel as you took that step?

10. What lessons would you share with others about your experience in doing so?

11. What additional steps will you take in the future?

Week Two Memory Verse

"Follow Me, and I will make you fishers of men." (Matthew 4:19, NKJV)

Week Three: Days One and Two

Improve Your Goals

... [A]s the Lord has called each one,
so let him walk.

— 1 Corinthians 7:17 (NKJV)

Throughout the lessons in *Disciple*, you have been gaining experiences that may have caused you to think differently about your life. For example, in days three and four of week two of Part One, you considered why God might have created your characteristics. During the lessons in Part Two, Live the Gospel, your love for others and interest in doing good probably increased. During Part Three, Draw Closer to Our Heavenly Father, the Lord Jesus Christ, and the Holy Spirit, you may have begun assigning a greater priority to spending time with God and meditating on Him and His Word. In this part of *Disciple*, you may have perceived more and better ways to help expand and improve God's Kingdom. Because of such changed perceptions resulting from these experiences, you now see what God wants you to accomplish differently and perhaps more clearly than when you began reading *Disciple*. In this lesson, you will take stock of those new perceptions to redefine and improve your goals to reflect God's calling on your life. 1 Corinthians 7:17 (NKJV) reminds us that God intends us to spend our time in accord with our individual callings.

Please note that I also addressed this lesson's subject in Lesson Three of *2,000 Percent Living* (Salvation Press, 2010). Feel free to read that material as well for a more detailed treatment of the subject.

Many people lack written goals for their lives. While such a lack enhances flexibility, such a lack can also encourage being too easily swayed by pressing, short-term demands that have little or nothing to do with your calling from God and what you, as a believer, should be doing. If you now use a thoughtful process for developing your goals, you will be more likely to do what God wants you to do.

Many people begin such goal setting by reading a secular book or attending a seminar led by someone who describes a logical process. I recommend, instead, that you pray for and seek God's guidance as the first step. Keep praying for such guidance as you proceed to consider options and finally to select goals.

As possible goals occur to you, I encourage you to test them for their spiritual significance to you and others. Doing so will help you avoid selecting one of many appealing goals that will not advance anyone's spiritual development. In addition, while God may have given you a heart to help a certain kind of person, testing spiritual relevance will help you to focus on goals that will enable you to be more fruitful in such helping.

Despite God's ability to make something good out of anything bad, wouldn't it be better to engage in goals that are more likely to produce only good results? To help with doing so, think about the worst possible results that could follow from your pursuit of a certain goal. For instance, having a larger home so you could host Christian events attended by more people could actually weaken your family if earning the needed money would cause you to be away from home much more often.

Once you think you have some good goals, I encourage you to review them with your Christian family members and friends to check for the goals' consistency with what God asks us to do as believers. After prayers and such comments have helped you to improve the goals' potential fruitfulness, then check with anyone else who will be affected, whether believer or not, to gain their ideas about the potential consequences of such goals. Such checking will enable you to avoid causing harm and hurt feelings as you prepare to launch off in what will probably be a somewhat different direction for your life.

Help Expand and Improve God's Kingdom by Improving Your Goals

Although it would be nice to be presented by the Holy Spirit with a list of what your goals should be, receiving such a list in this way seldom occurs. However, don't stop seeking God's guidance. As you consider and develop possible goals, get plenty of help. After you think you have the right goals, be sure to put them in order of importance, so that you will take the better or best of the possible actions when there are any conflicts. These questions will help you improve your goals so that you will become much more fruitful for God's Kingdom:

1. What aspects of serving God should be present in your goals?

2. How should achievement of these goals be defined, measured, and tracked?

3. About what do you need to be most careful in goal setting?

4. How can such goals be made less likely to result in any harm being done?

5. Who can help you improve each goal?

6. Who will want to be apprised of your thinking before you finalize the goals?

7. What should you do today to begin the goal-improvement process?

8. After receiving guidance from others and praying for direction, do you feel at peace?

9. What lessons would you share with others about your experience in improving your goals?

10. How will you monitor whether God wants you to add new goals and drop old ones?

Week Three Memory Verse

"… [A]s the Lord has called each one, so let him walk." (1 Corinthians 7:17, NKJV)

Week Three: Days Three and Four

Spend More Time on Your Most Fruitful Activities

"And do not seek what you should eat
or what you should drink,
nor have an anxious mind. For all these things
the nations of the world seek after, and
your Father knows that you need these things.
But seek the kingdom of God, and
all these things shall be added to you."

— Luke 12:29-31 (NKJV)

As a result of having improved goals for your life, you can become more productive for God's Kingdom. One way to accomplish such a fine result is by spending more time on your most fruitful activities for improving and expanding His Kingdom. The verses of Luke 12:29-31 (NKJV) present us with a remarkable promise: Seek God's Kingdom as your priority, and He will take care of your needs. Are you ready to rely on that promise? Doing so obviously requires faith, but you cannot build such faith without acting as if you already have it … and then seeing what God does.

The material in this lesson could be described in terms of putting first things (God's agenda) first. If you would like more detail for how to think about doing so, Lesson Four in *2,000 Percent Living* can be a helpful resource.

My experience has been that most people can increase how much time they spend on their most fruitful activities for God's agenda by more than 10 hours a week without sacrificing anything important. In part, that is because most people are spending so little time on such Godly activities. In part, it is because most people spend so much time on activities that are not part of God's agenda and do not play any useful role. While I do not know whether increased time spent in such ways will be at least 10 hours a week, I am sure it will be more than you expect unless you are already engaged in full-time ministry.

As part of prior lessons, you have already refocused your time. For instance, in days one and two of the second week in Part Three, you were encouraged to spend more time in prayer. On days one and two of the third week of the same part, you developed and began to follow a Bible-study routine. In the present part, you began to share your testimony more often.

Now, you should go beyond these fine beginnings. A useful next step is to keep track of how you spend all of your waking hours over the course of a typical week or two, assigning each activity to one of various categories such as work, commuting, household chores, watching television, surfing the Web, Bible study, prayer, attending church services, sharing the Gospel, volunteer work for Christian organizations, and various Kingdom activities. After adding the totals of times spent for each category of activity, assess that type's spiritual value. Activities such as prayer and Bible study would receive positive marks … while watching sit-coms on television would not.

Also, check your time spent in terms of how well it aligns with your new goals. You may be surprised to see how little, if any, time you currently spend on some of such goals.

Consider also when you are most productive at engaging in various activities. If you are like most people, you accomplish more at certain times of the day or on specific days of the week doing activities that require mental alertness and physical strength. In addition, you may need quiet conditions for some activities, such as Bible study, to be most fruitful. You should look, too, for when you are least productive for certain activities, especially those that are most closely related to your goals. When should you be doing each of your most important activities for God's Kingdom?

Finally, design a plan for spending your time to increase advancing your goals at the ideal times for doing so. As you do so, think of yourself as creating the life that God intended for you. As you plan these changes, don't burden yourself with more than you can handle. Instead, focus on unburdening yourself of whatever is holding you back from doing what would make you more fruitful. As part of doing so, consider how getting help from others could contribute to your increased fruitfulness.

Help Expand and Improve God's Kingdom by Spending More Time on Your Most Fruitful Activities

Our minds and bodies are better equipped in many cases to keep doing the same things than for shifting into better activities. Although the planning that occurs in this lesson will help to provide direction for shifting time spent towards more fruitful activities for God's Kingdom, you will also need His strength and encouragement to make and maintain the changes. Use your goals as a foundation for building your determination and attention to change. Stay in prayer about how to do so. The measurements and thinking described in this lesson for assessing where you are now in spending your time will probably help encourage making the necessary changes. The following questions are designed for making that self-assessment:

1. What are your most fruitful activities for helping to expand and improve God's Kingdom?

2. How much time did you spend on them yesterday? ... during the day before?

3. How much more time would you like to spend on those activities each day?

4. How might that increase be accomplished?

5. What shifts in the times when you engage in these activities should occur?

6. Who can help you make these changes?

7. What prayers will you make to gain direction, strength, and encouragement from God and others?

8. What should you do today to begin spending more time on your most fruitful activities?

9. How do the answers to these questions and spending more time on your most fruitful activities make you feel?

10. What lessons would you share with others about your experience just now in determining how to increase the time you will spend on your most fruitful activities?

11. How will you maintain a focus on increasing time spent on your most fruitful activities?

Week Three Memory Verse

"... [A]s the Lord has called each one, so let him walk." (1 Corinthians 7:17, NKJV)

Week Three: Days Five and Six

Reduce Time Spent on Unfruitful Activities

It happened in the spring of the year,
at the time when kings go out to battle,
that David sent Joab and his servants with him, and all Israel;
and they destroyed the people of Ammon and besieged Rabbah.
But David remained at Jerusalem.
Then it happened one evening that David arose from his bed and
walked on the roof of the king's house.
And from the roof he saw a woman bathing, and
the woman was *very beautiful to behold.*
So David sent and inquired about the woman.

— 2 Samuel 11:1-3 (NKJV)

2 Samuel 11:1-3 (NKJV) provides two examples of unfruitful activities that everyone should seek to avoid. First, David stayed in Jerusalem doing nothing, instead of something fruitful like leading Israel's army against God's enemies. Sloth can capture us, too, whether by spending an unneeded hour in bed, lazing on the couch watching junk television, or aimlessly wandering through a mall. Second, in the absence of doing what he should have been doing, David looked at what he should not have. As a result, he developed lust, later sinned with Bathsheba, and then arranged for her husband's death. The same drift into wickedness can happen to us by looking at something inappropriate on the Internet, indulging in an un-Godly activity, or playing with the idea of engaging in some sin.

Perhaps there is no better reminder to keep God in first place in our hearts, souls, and minds than considering how doing so prevents us from thinking and acting as we should not. When we realize that the time and effort that go into harmful activities could, instead, be used for fruitful ones, the full extent of lost fruitfulness can be more obvious to us.

Of course, many things we do aren't actually harmful to God's Kingdom; they just aren't helpful to It. Think of such activities as being spiritually neutral. Such an activity might be a time-consuming hobby or personal interest during which our engagement has no spiritual impact on us or anyone else. These activities can seem harmless, but they do have a cost in terms of drawing us away from what would be fruitful.

As you think about both kinds of unfruitful activities, I'm sure that you appreciate how staying focused on God increases fruitfulness. Such a focus provides two other benefits for avoiding wasted time and effort. First, mentally switching from activities not related to God's agenda to then doing something fruitful requires some time before you are again operating at full effectiveness. Second, you could become distracted by something else during any attempt to refocus on what your goals call you to do. Notice that neither problem occurs if you are always paying attention to God's agenda.

Measuring how you spend your time now as part of the prior lesson can help you identify where you are involved with either spiritually harmful or neutral activities. Obviously, do seek to eliminate both … but pay the most attention to the spiritually harmful ones. Then be sure to use any time that becomes available to increase your fruitful activities.

Help Expand and Improve God's Kingdom by Reducing Time Spent on Unfruitful Activities

For most people, forming a habit requires acting consistently in a different way for 30 to 45 days. If you are enthused about spending more time on fruitful activities, your emotional reaction can sufficiently sustain you to reduce any unfruitful activities identified by measuring how you spend time now. Because temptation to do such unfruitful activities will be strong for a longer time, stay in prayer to gain the strength and constancy to overcome any such temptations. As with the prior lesson, a self-assessment of your current situation will encourage you to make necessary changes even before the time-measurement results of the prior lesson are available. The following questions are designed for this more immediate self-assessment:

1. What are your activities that either harm God's Kingdom or have no effect on expanding and improving It?

2. How much time did you spend on those activities yesterday? … during the day before?

3. How much less time would you like to spend on those activities each day?

4. How might any decrease be accomplished?

5. What shifts in what you do can help you to make these changes?

6. Who can help you make these changes?

7. What prayers will you make to assist you?

8. How do the answers to these questions make you feel?

9. What should you do today to begin spending less time on your unfruitful activities?

10. What lessons would you share with others about your experience just now in determining how to decrease the time you will spend on unfruitful activities?

11. How can you prevent increasing time spent on unfruitful activities in the future?

Week Three Memory Verse

"… [A]s the Lord has called each one, so let him walk." (1 Corinthians 7:17, NKJV)

Week Four: Days One and Two

Learn More Fruitful Ways

The apostles, the elders, and the brethren,
To the brethren who are of the Gentiles
in Antioch, Syria, and Cilicia:
Greetings.

Since we have heard that some who went out from us
have troubled you with words, unsettling your souls, saying,
"You must be circumcised and keep the law" —
to whom we gave no such commandment —
it seemed good to us, being assembled with one accord,
to send chosen men to you
with our beloved Barnabas and Paul,
men who have risked their lives
for the name of our Lord Jesus Christ.
We have therefore sent Judas and Silas,
who will also report the same things by word of mouth.
For it seemed good to the Holy Spirit, and to us,
to lay upon you no greater burden than these necessary things:
that you abstain from things offered to idols,
from blood, from things strangled, and
from sexual immorality. If you keep yourselves from these,
you will do well.

Farewell.

— Acts 15:23-29 (NKJV)

While God can enhance whatever work you do with His supernatural resources, remember that the parables of Jesus are filled with examples of faithful people doing their best with the natural means at their disposal. Since Jesus gave His all on the cross for us, shouldn't we also do the best we can with whatever He has provided? Then, should supernatural resources be added, still more fruit will be produced.

In Acts 15:23-29 (NKJV), we see an example of believers in Jesus looking for ways to make witnessing more fruitful while remaining in accord with God's truth. There had been a dispute in the church about whether all the Old Testament requirements had to be observed, in addition to believing in and following Jesus as Lord and Savior. Unity among believers is important, as Jesus had continually reminded His disciples. Following Jesus was going to be a lot more appealing to potential converts if His people (especially those who weren't Israelites) did not have to observe all of the Mosaic laws, which included circumcision for males. Jesus had indicated while with the disciples that the teachings of the scribes and rabbis concerning the Law were not always correct. For instance, healing could be done on the Sabbath, even though the religious "experts" thought that was prohibited "work." As in this example, Jesus had emphasized acting in terms of the spirit of the Law, rather than in the narrow fulfillment of the mere words or to create a certain impression on others. In addition, Jesus added commandments that were not in the Mosaic Law, such as loving others as He loves us.

So how are we to proceed in learning more fruitful ways? This lesson's topic is a large one, connected to more opportunities than can be adequately explained in a few words. Let me point you to lessons five through fourteen in *2,000 Percent Living* as valuable resources for expanding your understanding of how fruitfulness in applying your spiritual gifts and talents can be greatly increased.

First, keep in mind that you don't have to reinvent the wheel to become more fruitful: Be a student of what others have done that has been highly fruitful. You should read about, observe, and speak with people who engage in such practices.

Second, learn how to use some of the most highly fruitful methods developed through The 400 Year Project to accomplish whatever God calls you to do. Such methods might include developing and implementing 2,000 percent solutions (ways of accomplishing at least 20 times more with the same or less time, effort, and resources) for an individual aspect of fruitfulness, repeatedly developing improved versions of such solutions in the same areas of fruitfulness, producing complementary 2,000 percent solutions (combining such fruitful solutions in ways such that their fruitfulness is multiplied by the improvements in the other complementary solutions), and launching excellent solutions (single sets of changes that create as much fruitfulness as 10 complementary 2,000 percent solutions). *Your Breakthroughs* (400 Year Project Press, 2016) by me can also provide background information about these opportunities.

Third, teach others to be highly fruitful by applying some of these same methods.

Fourth, identify how to be more active in performing such activities.

Help Expand and Improve God's Kingdom by Learning More Fruitful Ways

Many people assume that they already know enough to do almost anything well. Be at least a little more open minded and humble by asking God if you should learn any more fruitful ways. After all, Jesus had to restrain His disciples on several occasions from doing what they thought He wanted. Perhaps you will be redirected in some ways, as well. Below are some questions that may help you gain a better understanding of the likely benefits of learning more fruitful ways:

1. How did you learn to be fruitful in the activities you do now to expand and improve God's Kingdom?

2. How else could you learn to be fruitful in these regards?

3. What might be the benefits of such learning?

4. In what activities would you like to be more fruitful?

5. What are some ways you might learn to do so?

6. Who can help you learn?

7. What prayers will you make to gain God's directions?

8. How do the answers to these questions make you feel?

9. What should you do today to begin learning how to be more fruitful?

10. What lessons will you share with others about your experience just now in considering the opportunities to learn how to be more fruitful?

11. What will you do to continually enhance your fruitfulness?

Week Four Memory Verse

"Judge not, that you be not judged." (Matthew 7:1, NKJV)

Week Four: Days Three and Four

Engage in More Fruitful Ways and Experience Receiving More Than You Give

Jesus said to him,
"If you can believe, all things are possible to him who believes."

Immediately the father of the child cried out and said with tears,
"Lord, I believe; help my unbelief!"

— Mark 9:23-24 (NKJV)

Learning to be more fruitful is a wonderful and helpful activity. However, relatively little will be gained for expanding and improving God's Kingdom if you merely learn how to be more fruitful. Be sure to actually apply what you learn. Hopefully, you had some opportunities to do so as part of the process of learning more fruitful ways to serve God's Kingdom.

Many people interpret what Jesus said in Mark 9:23 (NKJV) as indicating that God will provide supernatural support to supply Godly results for someone who adequately believes in the possibility. Since what ensued involved the supernatural healing of a child afflicted with an evil spirit, that view is certainly valid. However, it is possible that Jesus *also* meant that our faith is valuable for helping us accomplish what we can do without supernatural support.

I often see belief play an important role in helping those who are quite skilled at using highly fruitful methods to accomplish more for expanding and improving God's Kingdom. While those who apply what they learn are almost always very successful, most of such people eventually lose interest in and confidence in their ability to repeat the success in the same or another area. Despite this lack of faith among many, the relatively few people who seek to repeatedly apply the highly fruitful methods they have used always create much more impact during the second or third time than by the first one, simply due to having developed valuable skills, experience, and knowledge during the initial effort.

Now that you have drawn much closer to God than you were when you began reading and applying the lessons in *Disciple*, I pray that you will continually seek His guidance and encouragement to become much more fruitful in your activities to expand and improve God's Kingdom. After all, He has given you access to great methods to apply, as described in the prior lesson. As they say in tennis, "The ball is now in your court." Will you act for Him today ... and every day?

By acting, you will probably experience a nice surprise: receiving more than you give on at least some occasions. Let me help you understand this possibility by contrasting it with the typical experience of helping someone either at home or at work. When someone asks for your help, or you see something that needs doing that no one is paying any attention to, you could be busy with other pressing tasks. Despite the disruption to your agenda, you probably help out. After you do so, you may receive a word of thanks for what you did. However, such appreciation will seldom amount to more than a quick "Thank you." When that happens, do you feel rewarded for your effort? Perhaps you do, but perhaps you don't.

Let me contrast such experiences with taking on a task for God to expand and improve His Kingdom. First, your choice of doing so will usually be voluntary. Second, you will probably be able to schedule doing so when there will be the fewest distractions. Third, when you complete the task, the Holy Spirit will infuse you with good feelings from God for your faithfulness. Fourth, God will reward you here on Earth and possibly for all eternity for what you do, as can be seen in Jesus' parables of the Minas and Talents. Fifth, your highly fruitful results will provide you with a sense of a job well done. Sixth, the results of what you do will go on forever by affecting lives that will influence still more lives and so forth, providing you with a daily opportunity to observe and enjoy having accomplished good results for Him. I could go on to point out more possible rewards, but I am sure by now you realize that serving God is more rewarding in many ways than even greatly serving any individual human, no matter who that person is or how the service is done.

Why am I so sure? Well, those I have taught how to apply the most fruitful methods have usually continued to apply them if their initial application was to expand and improve God's Kingdom, while those who merely used the methods to make more money or gain some personal advantage quickly lost interest. What's the difference? It's much more rewarding to serve Him than to serve yourself.

Help Expand and Improve God's Kingdom by Engaging in More Fruitful Ways and Experience Receiving More than You Give

Many believers assume that it's someone else's job to help the Kingdom advance in major ways. Since the Bible is filled with examples of ordinary people (such as uneducated shepherds and fishermen) who were called to do extraordinary things, I believe that God potentially has major roles for each of us to do His work. If few are being fruitful in such ways, it is often because few are choosing to follow Him to do what can be done, rather than because God doesn't want to team up with everyone who is willing to do more. Here are questions that may help you gain enthusiasm and determination to do more for God's Kingdom:

1. What are some highly fruitful activities that you have done to expand and improve God's Kingdom?

2. If you haven't done any, was your inaction a result of God telling you *not* to work on expanding and improving His Kingdom?

3. If you haven't done any, would you like to?

4. When you hear about ordinary people who have been very fruitful for God's Kingdom, what thoughts go through your mind?

5. If you have done one or more highly fruitful activity for His Kingdom, how did doing so make you feel?

6. What benefits did you gain?

7. Which of those benefits were unexpected?

8. What fruitful activities for God's Kingdom do you feel called to do that you haven't yet started?

9. Who can tell you what it's like to do such activities?

10. How do the answers to these questions make you feel?

11. What will you do today to start engaging in a new highly fruitful activity for expanding and improving God's Kingdom?

12. What lessons would you share with others about your experience just now in considering the opportunities to engage in more fruitful ways?

13. How will your future activities shift for being more fruitful in expanding and improving God's Kingdom?

<u>Week Four Memory Verse</u>

"Judge not, that you be not judged." (Matthew 7:1, NKJV)

Week Four: Days Five and Six

Track Your Fruitfulness and Praise God for Making It Possible

"For with what judgment you judge, you will be judged; and with the measure you use, it will be measured back to you."

— Matthew 7:2 (NKJV)

Matthew 7:2 (NKJV) should be read in conjunction with Matthew 7:1 (NKJV), which advises us not to judge. In the context of this lesson, however, let me suggest that we should look at the consequences of *what we do* with great care ... *and* from God's perspective. Everything we know from the Bible of what Jesus said is relevant to either expanding or improving God's Kingdom. Even when He complained about hypocrites and evil doers, the motive for doing so was to point out that such individuals' acts were blocking the Kingdom's expansion and development.

While only God can know the exact fruitfulness that occurs following an action we take, trying to understand what the results have been and could be for His Kingdom can be useful for better serving Him in these four ways:

1. First, seeing the results can help us identify how we can adjust what we do to accomplish more for the Kingdom.
2. Thinking about the impact can encourage us to take more of the most fruitful actions.
3. We can become inspired to find new, highly fruitful ways to expand and increase God's Kingdom.
4. Our example can inspire others to act in ways that they might not have otherwise done.

One of the important lessons I've learned from trying to take God's perspective is how little things He has directed me to do have often had large, positive consequences for the Kingdom. As a result, I am now very attentive to doing even very tiny things that the Holy Spirit brings to my attention. Even the smallest seed (as Jesus reminded us with the Parable of the Mustard Seed, Matthew 13:31-32, NKJV) can create something that will become great and have large impact. So I use Jesus' measure to think of all my actions as being like seeds for the Kingdom. Not only does doing so motivate me to plant more such seeds, but this perspective means I pay more attention to the results. Noticing any related fruitfulness further increases my joy and enthusiasm for doing more.

Watching such results has had an even more important consequence: I have come to appreciate even more about how great God is. Seeing Him use what little I have done to accomplish something substantial has made me better appreciate how powerful and good He is, as well as how amazing His plans are. As a result, I now praise Him with more understanding of who He is than I would if I had simply relied on my general impression of His greatness from reading the Bible.

Such praise also does something quite wonderful for me: It helps me to shrink my exaggerated self-image closer to its proper size. When compared to God, I'm very little in every dimension … except in my need for His guidance and help.

Help Expand and Improve God's Kingdom by Tracking Your Fruitfulness and Praising God for Making It Possible

While the most observant believers are usually quick to notice their mistakes and sins and then to ask God for forgiveness, relatively fewer of these believers regularly look into the fruitful results of what they have done for God's Kingdom and praise Him for enabling such results to occur. One way to begin expanding your attention and praise in this way is by looking at the consequences of your past actions for the Kingdom. The following questions are intended to help you do so:

1. What actions have you taken to either expand or improve God's Kingdom?

2. What have been the results so far?

3. What future results are likely to occur, as well?

4. How did God aid you in taking the actions?

5. How did God multiply their fruitfulness beyond the immediate impact of what you did?

6. What benefits did you gain?

7. Which of your benefits were unexpected?

8. How does it make you feel to consider His impact on your actions for the Kingdom?

9. How would you like to praise Him now?

10. What fruitful activities for God's Kingdom do you now feel called to do that you haven't yet started?

11. Who can tell you what it's like to do such activities?

12. How do the answers to these questions make you feel?

13. What will you do today to be more active in expanding and improving God's Kingdom?

14. What lessons would you share with others about your experience just now in thinking about the results of fruitful actions you have taken?

15. What will you do differently in the future as a result of answering these questions?

Week Four Memory Verse

"Judge not, that you be not judged." (Matthew 7:1, NKJV)

Week Five: Days One and Two

Consider if Parts of Your Calling Are Unfulfilled

"Blessed are *those who*
hunger and thirst for righteousness,
For they shall be filled.
Blessed are *the merciful,*
For they shall obtain mercy.
Blessed are *the pure in heart,*
For they shall see God.
Blessed are *the peacemakers,*
For they shall be called sons of God."

— Matthew 5:6-9 (NKJV)

Many discussions about relating to God divide the possibilities for doing so into two categories: being with Him in ways that enhance our relationship, or doing things either for Him or His Kingdom. While this categorization can certainly be applied to many choices, such as distinguishing between praying and sweeping up after a church service, there's also available a third category: activities that build a relationship with Him while also serving Him or His Kingdom. When considered from this third perspective, each of us can probably find more opportunities to grow spiritually *and* to be more fruitful.

As a starting point for being active from such a perspective, Jesus' words in Matthew 5:6-9 (NKJV) can be helpful. Almost every believer I know refers longingly at times to some way that the world needs more righteousness. The unfair treatment of certain individuals is a frequent example. At other times, many of these believers mention someone who has done wrong, but who should nevertheless be treated mercifully. On still other occasions, the sinfulness of the world is talked about in sad terms. Finally, almost all believers agree that more peace is needed. Obviously, the Holy Spirit has been busily at work in the hearts of all such individuals to encourage such concerns and desires.

While Jesus clearly indicated that such desires are good, He also talked about acting to advance the reality of what is desired, such as by being merciful, purifying one's own heart, and acting as a peacemaker. Your unique characteristics probably include greater sensitivity to noticing some needs for expanding and improving God's Kingdom than some other needs. God may have intended you to do something about changing what is wrong that most bothers you … and doing so in concert with and by building your relationship with Him, as well as by acting with His support.

What have you wanted to see improved that still needs improvement? Has God called you to be part of the solution? How have you acted on that call? Have you done enough?

Help Expand and Improve God's Kingdom by Considering if Parts of Your Calling Are Unfulfilled

Many believers have thoughtfully considered if they are doing enough to accomplish results for God, as well as if they are spending enough time with Him. What many of such believers have not yet done is examine their hearts to see if they have strong, unfulfilled desires to accomplish important results for God's Kingdom that could be sought in conjunction with God through prayers, seeking His guidance, sharing His love, expanding righteousness, being merciful, becoming purer, and helping make peace. With the following questions, you will determine if parts of your calling to expand and improve God's Kingdom include taking actions in any areas that you haven't yet addressed:

1. What un-Godly aspects of the world cause your strong disapproval?

2. What do you think needs to be done to reduce these aspects or their influence?

3. How do you feel called to participate in doing so?

4. What parts of that calling have you not yet acted on?

5. How could you work with God to be highly fruitful in these aspects of your calling?

6. Who can tell you how and what it's like to be highly fruitful in such activities?

7. In parts of the calling that you have acted on, could you do more?

8. In parts of the calling that you have acted on, could you be more fruitful?

9. How do the answers to these questions make you feel?

10. What will you do today to start accomplishing unfulfilled parts of your calling for expanding and improving God's Kingdom?

11. What lessons would you share with others about your experience just now in thinking about possible unfulfilled aspects of your calling from God?

12. What will you do differently in the future about these unfulfilled parts of your calling?

Week Five Memory Verse

"My grace is sufficient for you, for My strength is made perfect in weakness." (2 Corinthians 12:9, NKJV)

Week Five: Days Three and Four

Seek to Fulfill More of Your Calling

"My grace is sufficient for you,
for My strength is made perfect in weakness."

— 2 Corinthians 12:9 (NKJV)

"Who? Me?" Such a reaction often follows a believer perceiving some great calling from God for her or his life. Those who respond in this way often do so because they are quite clear that they either don't know what to do … or correctly appreciate that they cannot expect to accomplish much through their own efforts. Both reactions are accurate and understandable. However, such considerations are the wrong way to think about a calling: It's *not* about you … *it's about God.* Since He can do anything, it doesn't matter what you can or cannot do by yourself. He can do whatever else is required, and He knows exactly what to do. What the Lord said to the Apostle Paul in 2 Corinthians 12:9 (NKJV) directs us in how we should think when considering parts of our calling that seem way beyond us.

Think from God's perspective about your being weak for and ineffective in engaging in a Kingdom task. As a consequence, will you pay more attention to His directions as you follow Him? I sure hope so! Will others be more impressed that He exists and had a large hand in the good results? I don't see how they could help but have such a reaction, unless you persuaded them that God played no role, a very sinful, unlikely, and difficult thing to do. Will you want to draw closer to Him? Unless you are foolish, you certainly will. With just these few perspectives, you may begin to better appreciate more of the reasons why God often fills us with desires that involve performing what we are very poor at doing.

Can you act in faith that if God gave you a desire to accomplish something for His Kingdom, He also has a way to use and make highly fruitful whatever you can do? If not, you need more faith.

Help Expand and Improve God's Kingdom by Seeking to Fulfill More of Your Calling

In the prior lessons in this part of *Disciple*, you became more aware of how well God can use whatever you do for His Kingdom. You may also have discovered that you haven't been taking full advantage of the opportunities available to accomplish what's in your heart to do for Him. In this lesson, I hope you will discover that not doing what He has called you to do shows lack of faith and trust in God. Don't miss the opportunity to increase your faith and trust by repeatedly taking on what seems impossible to you! Your answers to the following questions will enable you to engage in and fulfill more of your calling:

1. What makes you think you should *not* engage in more aspects of what God has called you to do?

2. How does God answer when you bring these reasons to Him in prayer?

3. What does your inaction say about your faith in Him?

4. What does your inaction say about your trust in Him?

5. What does your inaction say about your relationship with Him?

6. What role does pride in making a good impression on others play in your inaction?

7. What role does your desire for comfort play in not being obedient to all parts of your calling?

8. Would Jesus have gone to the cross if He had thought about His calling the way you do yours?

9. How do the answers to these questions make you feel?

10. What will you do today to start accomplishing unfulfilled parts of your calling for expanding and improving God's Kingdom?

11. What lessons would you share with others about your experience just now in thinking about seeking to fulfill more of your calling from God?

12. What will you do differently in the future?

Week Five Memory Verse

"My grace is sufficient for you, for My strength is made perfect in weakness." (2 Corinthians 12:9, NKJV)

Week Five: Days Five and Six

Disciple Others

And Jesus came and spoke to them, saying,
"All authority has been given to Me in heaven and on earth.
Go therefore and make disciples of all the nations,
baptizing them in the name of the Father and
of the Son and of the Holy Spirit,
teaching them to observe all things that I have commanded you;
and lo, I am with you always,
even to the end of the age."

— Matthew 28:18-20 (NKJV)

Give instruction to a wise man, and he will be still wiser;
Teach a just man, and he will increase in learning.

— Proverbs 9:9 (NKJV)

The above verses state or imply three points that are the core of this lesson:

1. Jesus commanded making disciples of all nations, teaching them to observe His commands after they become believers.
2. As a believer gains accurate spiritual knowledge, she or he will grow in wisdom and learning.
3. Instruction concerning the commands of Jesus will advance believers in their spiritual development so they can accomplish more for God's Kingdom.

I can add nothing valuable to what these verses say.

As my final observation in this lesson, I encourage you to consider whatever benefits and blessings you have gained from believers teaching you to observe Jesus' commandments. With those benefits and blessings in mind, think about how sharing what you now know can help someone who hasn't yet learned the same things to become more fruitful. I strongly suspect that doing so is part of your calling from God. Pray about that.

Help Expand and Improve God's Kingdom by Discipling Others

In the prior 59 lessons, you were the beneficiary of texts designed to help you draw closer to God and to do more of what He wants you to do. In this final lesson, you encounter one more task that you may have been ignoring: helping other believers to draw closer to God and do more of what He wants them to do. You're answers to the following questions are designed to help you more fully and adequately do this task:

1. What was good about how you were discipled prior to reading *Disciple*?

2. What could have been improved about such discipleship?

3. How important has been such learning to developing your relationship with God and helping you to become more fruitful?

4. What would you like other believers to learn about developing their relationships with God and their becoming more fruitful?

5. How could you help such learning to occur?

6. What have you done so far to disciple others?

7. How do you feel about what you have and haven't done in this regard?

8. What does any inaction say about your relationship with Him?

9. Have you repented and asked for forgiveness for any inaction in this regard?

10. How do the answers to these questions make you feel?

11. What will you do today to start discipling believers?

12. What lessons would you like to share about your experience just now in thinking about doing more to disciple others?

13. What will you do differently in the future to disciple believers?

Week Five Memory Verse

"My grace is sufficient for you, for My strength is made perfect in weakness." (2 Corinthians 12:9, NKJV)

Thanks for faithfully engaging with *Disciple* through the 60 lessons. I pray that doing so has blessed you and God's Kingdom in many wonderful ways. If you have thoughts, questions, or suggestions for me, I hope you will contact me via e-mail at donmitchell@fastforward400.com/. May God bless you, your family, and all you do in the name of Jesus!

Appendix A

Jesus' Commands and Statements Implying Commands

Focusing on Jesus' commands is very important because He directed His disciples to teach future disciples to "observe all things that I have commanded you (Matthew 28:20, NKJV)." While Jesus taught many things during His ministry, most of them were not commands. Many of them were either descriptions of God's Kingdom, consequences of behavior, or promises. Reasonable people differ concerning how many commands Jesus gave that are in the New Testament. The following ones have attracted my attention because they appear to apply to everyone, not just to some people in some circumstances. While some of the following verses are statements of fact, to me they imply commands. If you prefer a different list, that's fine. I'm not claiming that this is the only possible list ... or even the list that He wants us to follow. I have ordered the verses in a way that makes a certain sense to me. Feel free to reorder the verses to emphasize a different sense.

"Repent, for the kingdom of heaven is at hand."

— Matthew 4:17 (NKJV)

"For the Father judges no one,
but has committed all judgment to the Son,
that all should honor the Son just as they honor the Father.
He who does not honor the Son
does not honor the Father who sent Him."

— John 5:22-23 (NKJV)

"If I do not do the works of My Father, do not believe Me;
but if I do, though you do not believe Me, believe the works,
that you may know and believe
that the Father is in Me, and I in Him."

— John 10:37-38 (NKJV)

"... [F]or if you do not believe that I am He,
you will die in your sins."

— John 8:24 (NKJV)

*"He who believes in Him is not condemned;
but he who does not believe is condemned already,
because he has not believed in
the name of the only begotten Son of God."*

— John 3:18 (NKJV)

*"Most assuredly, I say to you, unless one is born again,
he cannot see the kingdom of God."*

— John 3:3 (NKJV)

*"If anyone desires to come after Me,
let him deny himself, and take up his cross, and follow Me."*

— Matthew 16:24 (NKJV)

*"So likewise, whoever of you does not forsake all
that he has cannot be My disciple."*

— Luke 14:33 (NKJV)

*"If anyone serves Me, let him follow Me;
and where I am, there My servant will be also."*

— John 12:26 (NKJV)

*"Come to Me, all you who labor and are heavy laden,
and I will give you rest.
Take My yoke upon you and learn from Me,
for I am gentle and lowly in heart,
and you will find rest for your souls.
For My yoke is easy and My burden is light."*

— Matthew 11:28-30 (NKJV)

"Rejoice!"

— Matthew 28:9 (NKJV)

And as they were eating, Jesus took bread, blessed and broke it,
and gave it to the disciples and said,
"Take, eat; this is My body."

Then He took the cup, and gave thanks, and gave it to them, saying,
"Drink from it, all of you. For this is My blood of the new covenant,
which is shed for many for the remission of sins."

— Matthew 26:26-28 (NKJV)

"Whoever eats My flesh and drinks My blood has eternal life,
and I will raise him up at the last day.
For My flesh is food indeed, and My blood is drink indeed.
He who eats My flesh and drinks My blood
abides in Me, and I in him.
As the living Father sent Me, and I live because of the Father,
so he who feeds on Me will live because of Me."

— John 6:54-57 (NKJV)

"Go home to your friends, and tell them
what great things the Lord has done for you, and
how He has had compassion on you."

— Mark 5:19 (NKJV)

"As the Father loved Me,
I also have loved you;
abide in My love.
If you keep My commandments,
you will abide in My love,
just as I have kept My Father's commandments
and abide in His love.
These things I have spoken to you,
that My joy may remain in you, and
that your joy may be full."

— John 15:9-10 (NKJV)

"Abide in Me, and I in you.
As the branch cannot bear fruit of itself,
unless it abides in the vine,
neither can you, unless you abide in Me.
I am the vine, you are the branches.

He who abides in Me, and I in him, bears much fruit;
for without Me you can do nothing.
If anyone does not abide in Me,
he is cast out as a branch and is withered;
and they gather them and throw them into the fire,
and they are burned.
If you abide in Me, and My words abide in you,
you will ask what you desire,
and it shall be done for you.
By this My Father is glorified,
that you bear much fruit;
so you will be My disciples."

— John 15:4-8 (NKJV)

"Most assuredly, I say to you,
if anyone keeps My word he shall never see death."

— John 8:51 (NKJV)

"I am the resurrection and the life.
He who believes in Me, though he may die, he shall live.
And whoever lives and believes in Me shall never die."

— John 11:25-26 (NKJV)

Then He said to them,
"Follow Me, and I will make you fishers of men."

— Matthew 4:19 (NKJV)

Then He taught them many things by parables,
and said to them in His teaching:

"Listen! Behold, a sower went out to sow.

"And it happened, as he sowed,
that some seed fell by the wayside; and
the birds of the air came and devoured it.

"Some fell on stony ground, where it did not have much earth,
and immediately it sprang up because it had no depth of earth.
But when the sun was up it was scorched,
and because it had no root it withered away.

*"And some seed fell among thorns;
and the thorns grew up and choked it, and it yielded no crop.*

*"But other seed fell on good ground and
yielded a crop that sprang up, increased and produced:
some thirtyfold, some sixty, and some a hundred."*

*And He said to them,
"He who has ears to hear, let him hear!"*

— Mark 4:2-9 (NKJV)

*"And as you go, preach, saying, 'The kingdom of heaven is at hand.'
Heal the sick, cleanse the lepers, raise the dead, cast out demons.
Freely you have received, freely give."*

— Matthew 10:7-8 (NKJV)

*"Behold, I give you the authority to trample on serpents and scorpions,
and over all the power of the enemy, and
nothing shall by any means hurt you.
Nevertheless do not rejoice in this, that the spirits are subject to you,
but rather rejoice because your names are written in heaven."*

— Luke 10:19-20 (NKJV)

*Then He said to His disciples,
"The harvest truly is plentiful, but the laborers are few.
Therefore pray the Lord of the harvest
to send out laborers into His harvest."*

— Matthew 9:37-38 (NKJV)

*"But you shall receive power when the Holy Spirit has come upon you;
and you shall be witnesses to Me in Jerusalem, and
in all Judea and Samaria, and to the end of the earth."*

— Acts 1:8 (NKJV)

*And Jesus came and spoke to them, saying,
"All authority has been given to Me in heaven and on earth.
Go therefore and make disciples of all the nations,
baptizing them in the name of the Father and*

of the Son and of the Holy Spirit,
teaching them to observe all things that I have commanded you; and
lo, I am with you always, even *to the end of the age."*

— Matthew 28:18-20 (NKJV)

"So likewise you, when you have done
all those things which you are commanded, say,
We are unprofitable servants.
We have done what was our duty to do."'

— Luke 17:10 (NKJV)

Jesus said to him,
"'You shall love the LORD *your God with all your*
heart, with all your soul, and with all your mind.'
This is the first and great commandment.
And the second is like it:
'You shall love your neighbor as yourself.'
On these two commandments hang all the Law and the Prophets."

— Matthew 22:37-40 (NKJV)

"God is Spirit, and those who worship Him
must worship in spirit and truth."

— John 4:24 (NKJV)

But he, wanting to justify himself, said to Jesus,
"And who is my neighbor?"

Then Jesus answered and said:
"A certain man went down from Jerusalem to Jericho, and
fell among thieves, who stripped him of his clothing,
wounded him, and departed, leaving him half dead.

"Now by chance a certain priest came down that road.
And when he saw him, he passed by on the other side.

"Likewise a Levite, when he arrived at the place,
came and looked, and passed by on the other side.

"But a certain Samaritan, as he journeyed, came where he was.
And when he saw him, he had compassion.
So he went to him *and bandaged his wounds, pouring on oil and wine;*
and he set him on his own animal, brought him to an inn,
and took care of him. On the next day, when he departed,
he took out two denarii, gave them *to the innkeeper, and said to him,*
'Take care of him; and whatever more you spend,
when I come again, I will repay you.'

"So which of these three do you think was neighbor
to him who fell among the thieves?"

And he said, "He who showed mercy on him."

Then Jesus said to him, "Go and do likewise."

— Luke 10:29-37 (NKJV)

"A new commandment I give to you, that you love one another;
as I have loved you, that you also love one another.
By this all will know that you are My disciples,
if you have love for one another."

— John 13:34-35 (NKJV)

"Therefore, whatever you want men to do to you,
do also to them, for this is the Law and the Prophets."

— Matthew 7:12 (NKJV)

Then He also said to him who invited Him,
"When you give a dinner or a supper,
do not ask your friends, your brothers,
your relatives, nor rich neighbors,
lest they also invite you back, and you be repaid.
But when you give a feast, invite
the poor, *the* maimed, *the* lame, *the* blind.
And you will be blessed, because they cannot repay you;
for you shall be repaid at the resurrection of the just."

— Luke 14:12-14 (NKJV)

*"… [L]ove your enemies, bless those who curse you,
do good to those who hate you, and
pray for those who spitefully use you and persecute you,
that you may be sons of your Father in heaven …."*

— Matthew 5:44-45 (NKJV)

*Then He said to them, "Take heed what you hear.
With the same measure you use, it will be measured to you;
and to you who hear, more will be given.
For whoever has, to him more will be given;
but whoever does not have,
even what he has will be taken away from him."*

— Mark 4:24-25 (NKJV)

"To him who strikes you on the one *cheek,
offer the other also.
And from him who takes away your cloak,
do not withhold* your *tunic either."*

*"But if you love those who love you,
what credit is that to you?
For even sinners love those who love them."*

— Luke 6:29, 32 (NKJV)

*"Let your light so shine before men,
that they may see your good works and
glorify your Father in heaven."*

— Matthew 5:16 (NKJV)

*"Sell what you have and give alms;
provide yourselves money bags which do not grow old,
a treasure in the heavens that does not fail,
where no thief approaches nor moth destroys.
For where your treasure is, there your heart will be also."*

— Luke 12:33-34 (NKJV)

*"Take heed and beware of covetousness,
for one's life does not consist
in the abundance of the things he possesses."*

— Luke 12:15 (NKJV)

*"No servant can serve two masters;
for either he will hate the one and love the other,
or else he will be loyal to the one and despise the other.
You cannot serve God and mammon."*

— Luke 16:13 (NKJV)

*"Render therefore to Caesar the things that are Caesar's,
and to God the things that are God's."*

— Matthew 22:21 (NKJV)

*"Then the King will say to those on His right hand,
'Come, you blessed of My Father,
inherit the kingdom prepared for you
from the foundation of the world:
for I was hungry and you gave Me food;
I was thirsty and you gave Me drink;
I was a stranger and you took Me in;
I was naked and you clothed Me;
I was sick and you visited Me;
I was in prison and you came to Me.'*

*"Then the righteous will answer Him, saying,
'Lord, when did we see You hungry and feed You,
or thirsty and give You drink?
When did we see You a stranger and take You in,
or naked and clothe You?
Or when did we see You sick, or in prison, and come to You?'*

*"And the King will answer and say to them,
'Assuredly, I say to you, inasmuch as you did it
to one of the least of these My brethren, you did it to Me.'"*

— Matthew 25:34-40 (NKJV)

*"You call Me Teacher and Lord, and you say well, for so I am.
If I then, your Lord and Teacher, have washed your feet,
you also ought to wash one another's feet.
For I have given you an example,
that you should do as I have done to you.
Most assuredly, I say to you,
a servant is not greater than his master;
nor is he who is sent greater than he who sent him.
If you know these things, blessed are you if you do them."*

— John 13:13-17 (NKJV)

*"And do not seek what you should eat
or what you should drink,
nor have an anxious mind. For all these things
the nations of the world seek after, and
your Father knows that you need these things.
But seek the kingdom of God, and
all these things shall be added to you."*

— Luke 12:29-31 (NKJV)

*"Give to him who asks you, and
from him who wants to borrow from you do not turn away."*

— Matthew 5:42 (NKJV)

*"But when you do a charitable deed,
do not let your left hand know what your right hand is doing,
that your charitable deed may be in secret; and
your Father who sees in secret will Himself reward you openly."*

— Matthew 6:3-4 (NKJV)

*But Jesus said, "Let the little children come to Me,
and do not forbid them;
for of such is the kingdom of heaven."*

— Matthew 19:14 (NKJV)

"But you, do not be called 'Rabbi';
for One is your Teacher, the Christ,
and you are all brethren.
Do not call anyone on earth your father;
for One is your Father,
He who is in heaven.
And do not be called teachers;
for One is your Teacher, the Christ."

— Matthew 23:8-10 (NKJV)

"In this manner, therefore, pray:

Our Father in heaven,
Hallowed be Your name.
Your kingdom come.
Your will be done
On earth as it is in heaven.
Give us this day our daily bread.
And forgive us our debts,
As we forgive our debtors.
And do not lead us into temptation,
But deliver us from the evil one.
For Yours is the kingdom and the power
and the glory forever. Amen.

"For if you forgive men their trespasses,
your heavenly Father will also forgive you.
But if you do not forgive men their trespasses,
neither will your Father forgive your trespasses."

— Matthew 6:9-15 (NKJV)

"So I say to you, ask, and it will be given to you;
seek, and you will find; knock, and it will be opened to you.
For everyone who asks receives, and he who seeks finds,
and to him who knocks it will be opened.
If a son asks for bread from any father among you,
will he give him a stone? Or if he asks for a fish,
will he give him a serpent instead of a fish?
Or if he asks for an egg, will he offer him a scorpion?
If you then, being evil, know how to give good gifts to your children,
how much more will your heavenly Father
give the Holy Spirit to those who ask Him!"

— Luke 11:9-13 (NKJV)

"Ask, and you will receive, that your joy may be full."

— John 16:24 (NKJV)

Then He spoke a parable to them,
that men always ought to pray and not lose heart ....

— Luke 18:1 (NKJV)

"But you, when you fast, anoint your head and wash your face,
so that you do not appear to men to be fasting,
but to your Father who is *in the secret* place; *and*
your Father who sees in secret will reward you openly."

— Matthew 6:17-18 (NKJV)

"Judge not, and you shall not be judged.
Condemn not, and you shall not be condemned.
Forgive, and you will be forgiven."

— Luke 6:37 (NKJV)

"Or how can you say to your brother,
'Brother, let me remove the speck that is *in your eye,'*
when you yourself do not see the plank that is *in your own eye?*
Hypocrite! First remove the plank from your own eye,
and then you will see clearly
to remove the speck that is in your brother's eye."

— Luke 6:42 (NKJV)

"Moreover if your brother sins against you,
go and tell him his fault between you and him alone.
If he hears you, you have gained your brother.
But if he will not hear, take with you one or two more,
that 'by the mouth of two or three witnesses
every word may be established.'
And if he refuses to hear them, tell it *to the church.*
But if he refuses even to hear the church,
let him be to you like a heathen and a tax collector."

— Matthew 18:15-17 (NKJV)

"I do not say to you, [forgive] up to seven times,
but up to seventy times seven."

— Matthew 18:22 (NKJV)

"Therefore be merciful, just as your Father also is merciful."

— Luke 6:36 (NKJV)

"Anyone who speaks a word against the Son of Man,
it will be forgiven him;
but whoever speaks against the Holy Spirit,
it will not be forgiven him,
either in this age or in the age to come."

— Matthew 12:32 (NKJV)

"Do not forbid him, for no one who works a miracle in My name
can soon afterward speak evil of Me.
For he who is not against us is on our side."

— Mark 9:39-40 (NKJV)

Then they understood that He did not tell them
to beware of the leaven of bread, but
of the doctrine of the Pharisees and Sadducees.

— Matthew 16:12 (NKJV)

"Beware of the leaven of the Pharisees, which is hypocrisy."

— Luke 12:1 (NKJV)

"The scribes and the Pharisees sit in Moses' seat.
Therefore whatever they tell you to observe, that observe and do,
but do not do according to their works;
for they say, and do not do."

— Matthew 23:2-3 (NKJV)

"But rather give alms of such things as you have;
then indeed all things are clean to you."

— Luke 11:41 (NKJV)

"Therefore if you bring your gift to the altar, and
there remember that your brother has something against you,
leave your gift there before the altar, and go your way.
First be reconciled to your brother, and
then come and offer your gift."

— Matthew 5:23-24 (NKJV)

And He said to those who sold doves,
"Take these things away!
Do not make My Father's house a house of merchandise!"

— John 2:16 (NKJV)

"You have heard that it was said to those of old,
'You shall not commit adultery.'
But I say to you that whoever looks at a woman to lust for her
has already committed adultery with her in his heart."

— Matthew 5:27-28 (NKJV)

"Whoever divorces his wife and marries another
commits adultery against her.
And if a woman divorces her husband and marries another,
she commits adultery."

— Mark 10:11-12 (NKJV)

"Again you have heard that it was said to those of old,
'You shall not swear falsely,
but shall perform your oaths to the Lord.'
But I say to you, do not swear at all:
neither by heaven, for it is God's throne;
nor by the earth, for it is His footstool;
nor by Jerusalem, for it is the city of the great King."

— Matthew 5:33-35 (NKJV)

*"Put your sword in its place,
for all who take the sword will perish by the sword."*

— Matthew 26:52 (NKJV)

*"Agree with your adversary quickly, while you are on the way with him,
lest your adversary deliver you to the judge,
the judge hand you over to the officer, and you be thrown into prison.
Assuredly, I say to you, you will by no means get out of there
till you have paid the last penny."*

— Matthew 5:25-26 (NKJV)

*"You have heard that it was said,
'An eye for an eye and a tooth for a tooth.'
But I tell you not to resist an evil person."*

— Matthew 5:38-39 (NKJV)

*"And I say to you, My friends,
do not be afraid of those who kill the body, and
after that have no more that they can do.
But I will show you whom you should fear:
Fear Him who, after He has killed,
has power to cast into hell;
yes, I say to you, fear Him!"*

— Luke 12:4-5 (NKJV)

*"In the world you will have tribulation;
but be of good cheer, I have overcome the world."*

— John 16:33 (NKJV)

*"Now when they bring you to the
synagogues and magistrates and authorities,
do not worry about how or what you should answer,
or what you should say. For the Holy Spirit will teach you
in that very hour what you ought to say."*

— Luke 12:11-12 (NKJV)

"Watch and pray, lest you enter into temptation.
The spirit indeed is willing, but the flesh is weak."

— Matthew 26:41 (NKJV)

"Take heed, watch and pray;
for you do not know when the time is [for Jesus' return]."

— Mark 13:33 (NKJV)

"Watch therefore, and pray always
that you may be counted worthy to escape
all these things [the Tribulation] that will come to pass, and
to stand before the Son of Man."

— Luke 21:36 (NKJV)

"Blessed are you when they revile and persecute you, and
say all kinds of evil against you falsely for My sake.
Rejoice and be exceedingly glad,
for great is your reward in heaven,
for so they persecuted the prophets who were before you."

— Matthew 5:11-12 (NKJV)

List of Verses Containing Jesus' Commands and Statements Implying Commands

— Matthew 4:17 (NKJV)
— Matthew 4:19 (NKJV)
— Matthew 5:11-12 (NKJV)
— Matthew 5:16 (NKJV)
— Matthew 5:23-24 (NKJV)
— Matthew 5:25-26 (NKJV)
— Matthew 5:27-28 (NKJV)
— Matthew 5:33-35 (NKJV)
— Matthew 5:38-39 (NKJV)
— Matthew 5:42 (NKJV)
— Matthew 5:44-45 (NKJV)
— Matthew 6:3-4 (NKJV)
— Matthew 6:9-15 (NKJV)
— Matthew 6:17-18 (NKJV)
— Matthew 7:12 (NKJV)
— Matthew 9:37-38 (NKJV)
— Matthew 10:7-8 (NKJV)

— Matthew 11:28-30 (NKJV)
— Matthew 12:32 (NKJV)
— Matthew 16:12 (NKJV)
— Matthew 16:24 (NKJV)
— Matthew 18:15-17 (NKJV)
— Matthew 18:22 (NKJV)
— Matthew 19:14 (NKJV)
— Matthew 22:21 (NKJV)
— Matthew 22:37-40 (NKJV)
— Matthew 23:2-3 (NKJV)
— Matthew 23:8-10 (NKJV)
— Matthew 25:34-40 (NKJV)
— Matthew 26:26-28 (NKJV)
— Matthew 26:41 (NKJV)
— Matthew 26:52 (NKJV)
— Matthew 28:9 (NKJV)
— Matthew 28:18-20 (NKJV)

— Mark 4:2-9 (NKJV)
— Mark 4:24-25 (NKJV)
— Mark 5:19 (NKJV)
— Mark 9:39-40 (NKJV)
— Mark 10:11-12 (NKJV)
— Mark 13:33 (NKJV)

— Luke 6:29, 32 (NKJV)
— Luke 6:36 (NKJV)
— Luke 6:37 (NKJV)
— Luke 6:42 (NKJV)
— Luke 10:19-20 (NKJV)
— Luke 10:29-37 (NKJV)
— Luke 11:9-13 (NKJV)
— Luke 11:41 (NKJV)
— Luke 12:1 (NKJV)
— Luke 12:4-5 (NKJV)
— Luke 12:11-12 (NKJV)
— Luke 12:15 (NKJV)
— Luke 12:29-31 (NKJV)
— Luke 12:33-34 (NKJV)
— Luke 14:12-14 (NKJV)
— Luke 14:33 (NKJV)
— Luke 16:13 (NKJV)
— Luke 17:10 (NKJV)
— Luke 18:1 (NKJV)
— Luke 21:36 (NKJV)

— John 2:16 (NKJV)
— John 3:3 (NKJV)

— John 3:18 (NKJV)
— John 4:24 (NKJV)
— John 5:22-23 (NKJV)
— John 6:54-57 (NKJV)
— John 8:24 (NKJV)
— John 8:51 (NKJV)
— John 10:37-38 (NKJV)
— John 11:25-26 (NKJV)
— John 12:26 (NKJV)
— John 13:13-17 (NKJV)
— John 13:34-35 (NKJV)
— John 15:4-8 (NKJV)
— John 15:9-10 (NKJV)
— John 16:24 (NKJV)
— John 16:33 (NKJV)

— Acts 1:8 (NKJV)

Appendix B

Donald Mitchell's Testimony

He will lift you up.

Humble yourselves
in the sight of the Lord,
and He will lift you up.

— James 4:10 (NKJV)

Let me share with you how I became a Christian so you will know where I am coming from with regard to encouraging you to become a Christian and to be fruitful in Godly contributions for creating and implementing breakthrough solutions to developing and expanding God's Kingdom.

There has been a long commitment to the Lord in our family. For example, I remember my great-grandmother, Edith Foster, reading the Bible every day. As a youngster, my mother usually took me to Sunday school. It was my least favorite activity; sleeping was much preferred. I did enjoy listening to sermons, but it was frowned on to take youngsters to the adult services where the sermons were given.

If I pretended to be asleep, mom would sometimes let me stay in bed on Sundays. I was pretty good at pretending, and I soon was the biggest backslider in my Sunday school grade. Fortunately, it was an evangelical church so my classmates were always cooking up schemes to get me to attend again. Because of my high opinion of myself, I would always return if invited to play my clarinet for the congregation.

By the time I turned thirteen, I was pretty full of myself. There wasn't much room for God in there alongside my exaggerated opinion of myself.

One day at home while my family was away for a drive, I felt really sick. By the time they returned, I was delirious. Within an hour, I was in the hospital where I would stay for two weeks as I barely survived a bad case of double pneumonia.

My physician, Dr. Helmsley, was an observant Christian and worried about my soul because my life was in jeopardy. He talked to me about our Heavenly Father, Jesus, and the Holy Spirit twice a day when he stopped by to check on me. These conversations were when I first learned how to become a Christian through being born again. I also came to realize that I couldn't stop sinning on my own. I needed a Savior, Jesus Christ! After I recovered, he took my mom and me to a tent revival meeting.

Having recovered from the illness, I soon pushed God out of my life again. During the next year, I was, instead, very caught up in athletics. When I was in ninth grade, I desperately wanted to make a contribution to our junior high track team, which had a remote chance of winning the big meet. Our coach, Mr. Layman, told each of us exactly what had to be accomplished for the team to win. I was determined to do my part. I had to come in first!

But that wasn't likely to happen. Based on past performances, there were at least two people who could out leap me in the standing broad jump, my main event. To make such a jump, you stand on a slightly raised, forward-tilted board and spring outward as far as you can into a sand-filled pit. After two of the three jumping rounds, I knew it was hopeless. I was in sixth place and four of the competitors' jumps were longer than I had ever gone before. I also didn't like the board we were using.

Remembering that we should call on God when we need help, I thought of praying … but what I wanted was so trivial in God's terms that I didn't think it was worthy of prayer. So I decided to make God an offer instead: "Dear God, help me win this event, and I'm yours forever." After all, if He came through, any doubts I had about God would be dispelled.

I stepped onto the broad-jump board and felt very calm. I did my routine and took off into the air. Instantly, I felt light as a feather cradled in a large, gentle hand that was lifting me. I was dropped softly at the far end of the pit. I had outleapt everyone and gone more than six inches past my best previous jump. I couldn't believe it. Then I remembered my promise to God, thanked Him, repented my sins, accepted Jesus as my Lord and Savior, and ran off to tell everyone on the team.

Even more remarkable, I was the only person on the team who performed up to the plan. Knowing what had to be done had probably given us performance anxiety, and people underperformed because they didn't believe they could do what the team needed. I also suspect that God wanted to make a point with me that I needed Him.

After a few days, I started to think that perhaps I'd just developed a new broad-jump technique and God didn't have a role at all. God soon dispelled that thought by making sure that my jumps for the rest of my life were much shorter than I had jumped when He lifted me up.

Since then, God has been speaking to me on a regular basis through the Holy Spirit. I have learned to pay attention and to act promptly. When I pursue my own ideas, things don't go so well. When I follow His directions, things work out great. That's my secret to high performance, and I just wanted to share it with you so you could benefit, too. He knows the answers, even when you and I don't … which is most of the time.

As a management consultant, the Holy Spirit has often filled me with knowledge about what the consequences of one set of actions would be compared to another for my clients. Naturally, I always recommended as the Holy Spirit directed me. Clients often told me that they were impressed by how certain I was of my conclusions and of how persuasive I could be in describing the advantages of whatever recommendations were made. Once again, the explanatory words came from the Holy Spirit, rather than from me.

Unfortunately, I wasn't comfortable in my younger days sharing my faith with clients, and I wrongly gave many people the impression that I was the author of the solutions rather than merely the transmitter.

I wish I had been more faithful in this regard. I apologize to my clients for having missed so many great witnessing opportunities. I didn't always listen as well as I should in making decisions that primarily affected me, but God would always do something to get my attention. Here's an example. I made an investment that I hoped would reduce my taxes in addition to making some money. I didn't have a good feeling from the Holy Spirit at the time, and I shouldn't have invested.

My tax return was later audited by the Internal Revenue Service concerning that investment. It turned out I was in the wrong for the deductions I had taken. Anticipating a big tax bill plus penalties and interest, you can imagine my astonishment when the revised tax return showed me owing no additional money to the government even though I had lost on the audit issues. I knew that result was a gift from God, and I was totally overwhelmed by His wisdom and power in protecting me. Praise God for His mercy!

I rededicated my life to Jesus in 1995, and I have enjoyed great peace since then. I have also done a lot better in being obedient to the Holy Spirit and to what the Bible tells us to do in all aspects of my life. Many blessings have been mine since then.

After being told by God to start The 400 Year Project (demonstrating how everyone in the world could make improvements 20-times faster and more effectively than normal with no additional resources) in 1995, I continued to receive His instructions. In 2005, for example, God told me to start explaining to people how to live their lives by gaining more joy from what they already have.

In the summer of 2006, I began to see how The 400 Year Project could be brought to a successful conclusion (as I reported in *Adventures of an Optimist*, Mitchell and Company Press, 2007). Realizing that perhaps I had devoted too much of my attention to this one challenge, I began to seek ways to rebalance my life. One of those rebalancing methods was to spend more time communing with God through prayer, Scriptural studies, attending church services and Bible classes, and listening more to the still, small voice within.

For several years I had been enjoying the devotionals sent to me daily over the Internet by evangelist Bill Keller. One of those devotionals speared me like an arrow that summer. The evangelist reminded his readers that our responsibility as believers is to share our faith with others through our example and sharing the Gospel message from the Bible. Not feeling well equipped to do more than try to be a good example, I began to pray about what else I should be doing.

The next day, my answer came: I was to launch a global contest to locate the most effective ways that souls were being saved and be sure that information was shared widely. This sharing would be a blessing for those who wished to fulfill the Great Commission to spread the Good News of Jesus as commanded in Matthew 28:18-20 (NKJV):

And Jesus came and spoke to them, saying, "All authority has been given to Me in heaven and on earth. Go therefore and make disciples of all the nations, baptizing them in the name of the Father and of the Son and of the Holy Spirit, teaching them to observe all things that I have commanded you; and lo, I am with you always, *even* to the end of the age."

The contest winners were Jubilee Worship Center in Hobart, Indiana, and Step by Step Ministries in Porter, Indiana. You can read their experiences to learn amazingly effective ways to help unsaved people choose to accept Salvation in *Witnessing Made Easy: Yes, You Can Make a Difference* (Jubilee Worship Center Step by Step Press, 2010) by Bishop Dale P. Combs, Lisa Combs, Jim Barbarossa, Carla Barbarossa, and me. Six other worthy ideas and practices from the contest for assisting more people to learn about and some to be moved by the Holy Spirit to pledge their lives to Jesus are described in *Ways You Can Witness: How the Lost Are Found* (Salvation Press, 2010) by Cherie Hill, Roger de Brabant, Drew Dickens, Gael Torcise, Wendy Lobos, Herpha Jane Obod, Gisele Umugiraneza, and me.

Let me tell you another interesting thing about my life with Jesus. When my daughter was about a year old, I suffered what resembled a stroke that caused me to start to become paralyzed. As I could feel my face's muscles freezing, I immediately prayed to Jesus to stop the paralysis and He did. I was left with a lot of pain and numbness on the left side of my body and was very weak for over a year.

Part of that pain continued for the next twenty-two years until, on November 8, 2009, I asked two of my pastors during a communion service to pray in the name of Jesus that the remaining pain be removed. During the prayer, the pain started leaving immediately and was totally gone within a half hour. As I felt the pain leaving me, through some power traveling inch by inch down my body, I was overcome with gratitude and fell on my knees in thanks.

That wasn't the only time He recently healed me. Encouraged by that miraculous experience, I came forward again on December 19, 2010, during another communion service to request prayer for relief from the pain in my wrists that was making it difficult for me to write books to serve Him and to do my other work. Knowing that my mother had been plagued with arthritis, I assumed it was a similar onset for me. My pastors were occupied with prayers for other members of the congregation. This time an elder of the church and his wife anointed me with oil and prayed for me. Almost immediately, I couldn't stop my body from violently shaking. Gradually, the shaking was reduced until it ceased after about half an hour, and my wrist pain was totally gone. It has not returned. I was even more overwhelmed that He had healed me again. Can anyone appreciate all the goodness that God has in store for us?

Let me share yet another miraculous healing (not the last that I've experienced). I've always been troubled with many respiratory and food allergies and sensitivities. In my sixties, these problems had become worse. I finally reached the point where it was difficult to be in the same room with another person due to my reactions to any deodorants and scents they were using. During still another communion service on January 16, 2012, two pastors again prayed for me to be relieved of these problems so that I could be a better witness for Him. Once again, power filled my body. My allergies and sensitivities were gone in a few minutes. Since then, they haven't returned. It has made a huge improvement in my life and in my witnessing.

I have also been saved by God from what I believed to be certain death on twelve occasions, most recently on July 2, 2013. I won't go into all of these events, but I did want you to be aware that He is always touching all aspects of my life in beneficial ways.

While it is up to God to decide if and when He wants to heal us or to protect us from harm, it is certainly reassuring to know that He has the ability and power to do anything He wants.

Glory be to God! Praise Him always! His miracles, grace, and mercy never end. I am so happy and honored to be His servant and witness to you.

Appendix C

Summary of The 400 Year Project

Therefore we also pray always for you
that our God would count you worthy of this calling,
and fulfill all the good pleasure of His goodness
and the work of faith with power,
that the name of our Lord Jesus Christ
may be glorified in you, and you in Him,
according to the grace of our God
and the Lord Jesus Christ.

— 2 Thessalonians 1:11-12 (NKJV)

One morning during the summer of 1995 at around 3:45 a.m., I felt a warm presence fill the bedroom. In response, my body temperature seemed to rise and I felt deliriously happy. A voice that I didn't recognize filled my mind and told me in tones that were more resonant and powerful than James Earl Jones on his best day that I should hold a meeting on the autumnal equinox for all of my management consulting clients to celebrate and share their greatest accomplishments. At the end of the meeting, I should announce that I would be starting a 20-year project to find ways for the whole world to make 400 years of normal progress in only 20 years, beginning in 2015 and finishing in 2035. For the next few weeks, I could think of little else.

What had happened? I prayed over the experience quite a bit and concluded that God had sent me a message. Why me? I have no idea. Maybe He couldn't find anyone else crazy enough to take on such an impossible task. I certainly felt that only God would know how to do it.

Why that time frame? I don't know, but it later occurred to me that the 2,000th anniversary of Jesus' crucifixion and resurrection would occur during 2015–2035. Perhaps that was an important connection. Since then, I have come to appreciate that 20 is a spiritually important number to God: Notice that the dimensions of the Holy of Holies in the Temple were measured in terms of 20 cubits. But who knows, except God?

How would I pursue this project? I had no idea, not even a clue. All I knew was that I was supposed to make this announcement at the autumnal equinox.

I quickly organized the meeting. Clients graciously agreed to fly in to share their triumphs and lessons with one another. Not knowing how anyone else would take the announcement of the new project, I decided to keep it to myself. I also had the impression that I should keep the project private until the announcement. Otherwise, why make the announcement then rather than sooner?

The event went much better than I could have hoped, especially since I wasn't sure what to say during the unexpected announcement. Almost everyone was encouraging, and many volunteered to help.

A key early focus was to engage in writing a book that Peter Drucker, the founder of the management discipline, had encouraged Carol Coles and me to write encapsulating a problem-solving method that we had been using for many years. We were fortunate to gain the assistance of Robert Metz, a veteran author and journalist, as a coauthor to lead us through the publication twists and turns. That book was *The 2,000 Percent Solution*, still the most widely read publication produced by The 400 Year Project.

Having experienced a warm reception for this book, I was delighted when the Holy Spirit kept providing concepts, processes, or the actual words for many future books, of which twenty-one more have been completed with the publication of *Disciple*. Through these books, readers and students of mine have created their own breakthroughs by employing The 400 Year Project's methods. I'm aware of successful demonstration projects that have been conducted so far in over 60 countries. There are probably more such successes that I'm unaware of. What a blessing! Praise God!

I have also had the pleasure of conducting several global contests, building experience to supplement the concepts first articulated in *The Ultimate Competitive Advantage* about this way of making rapid advances.

I also established a learning organization, The Billionaire Entrepreneurs' Master Mind, to advance how complementary 2,000 percent solutions could be most effectively developed and combined. The lessons developed by that group richly informed *Business Basics* and the three books in the Advanced Business series.

Today, The 400 Year Project is ready for prime time. The books, experiences, and networks of problem solvers provide a sound foundation for breakthroughs in expanding and transforming God's Kingdom in every possible dimension between now and 2035 by far more than 20 times. I am delighted that you will be part of creating such remarkable transformations.

May God bless you, your family, and all you do in the name of Jesus!

www.ingramcontent.com/pod-product-compliance
Lightning Source LLC
Chambersburg PA
CBHW080934040426
42443CB00015B/3409